The Full Vermonty

Vermont in the Age of Trump

The Full Vermonty
Vermont in the Age of Trump

❧

BILL MARES
&
JEFF DANZIGER

GREEN WRITERS PRESS
Brattleboro, Vermont

for Chris, forever

Printed in Vermont in the United States

10 9 8 7 6 5 4 3 2

Green Writers Press is a Vermont-based publisher whose mission is to
spread a message of hope and renewal through the words and images we
publish. We will adhere to our commitment to preserving and protecting
the natural resources of the earth. To that end, a percentage of our
proceeds will be donated to environmental and social-justice activist
groups. Green Writers Press gratefully acknowledges the generosity of
individual donors, friends, and readers to help support the environment
and our publishing initiative. For information about funding or getting
involved in our publishing program, contact Green Writers Press.

Giving Voice to Writers & Artists Who Will Make the World a Better Place
Green Writers Press | Brattleboro, Vermont
www.greenwriterspress.com

ISBN: 978-0999076606

Visit www.thefullvermonty.net for more hilarity & solidarity.

PRINTED IN VERMONT ON RECYCLED PAPER BY A FAMILY-OWNED PRINTER.

Acknowledgments

❧

First of all, we want to thank Dede Cummings, our publisher, for believing in the book from the beginning. We are also indebted to Mike Fleming, our excellent and expeditious editor. We thank our nineteen collaborators who all delivered *on deadline* their packets of anger and resolve, anguish and hilarity. In addition, we thank the following for their ideas and encouragement along the way: Chris Hadsel, Wolfgang Mieder, Bob McKearin, Gideon Danziger, Mimi Ross, Patrick Savage, Frank and Lee Bryan, Greg Cluff, Anne Galloway, and Tim and Nick Hadsel-Mares.

Contents

❧

Preface:
Vermont Stumps the Trump

BILL MARES

❧

S HORTLY AFTER I HAD OPEN HEART SURGERY, Donald
Trump's election was the nightmarish present I received on
my birthday. Like millions of other Democrats (and some
Republicans), I went into denial. How could 63 million people
be so wrong? During the campaign, I had reread the Sinclair
Lewis novel *It Can't Happen Here*, about a right-wing presiden-
tial victory. Little did I expect that this book, written and set in
Vermont in 1935, would be so prescient.

Now we would have a presidential buffoon, a man of willful
ignorance, bigotry, and prejudice, a malignant narcissist who
lacked all curiosity, compassion, and humility. Upon further
reflection, I saw that the Republicans had done it with the help
of Russian hacking, the antiquated electoral college, widespread
gerrymandering, and appeals to the worst human instincts.

As I recovered physically, I deteriorated mentally. I got
angrier and angrier. I couldn't march because of my heart. I had
no complaints to voice about our Vermont congressional delegation. Okay, I could dutifully write checks to the ACLU and
350.org. But it wasn't enough.

I sought comfort from my friends in Vermont and beyond.
Among them was Jeff Danziger, a cartoonist whom I have

known for forty years and who has illustrated four of my books. He splits his time between Vermont and New York City. With his biting political cartoons, he daily afflicts the comfortable and comforts the afflicted.

While we commiserated, he said, "Why not write another book before dementia sets in?"

I thought of what Rachel Maddow had said a few weeks earlier: "Think of what you do well, and do it for the country." I can write humor, but I told Jeff, "I'll only do it with you!"

Jeff came right back with "How about *The Full Vermonty: Vermont in the Age of Trump?*"

The next day, our idea still had luster. Jeff and I began to scour the hills and hollows for ideas. Vermont has withstood the Revolution, a New York invasion, and the New Hampshire Land Grants, and will assuredly survive the next few years under the Washington Axis of Evil, a.k.a. the Trump Administration, the Republicans in Congress, and conservatives on the Supreme Court.

Vermont was the first state to outlaw slavery. We banned billboards and went to great lengths to protect our natural resources. From Matthew Lyon to Ralph Flanders, Vermont has a history of speaking truth to tyranny. We're little but we're loud. Look how we elected a New Yorker, Bernie Sanders, to represent us in the United States Senate and carry our message nationwide.

Trump's cyclonic destruction of civic and political engagement continues unabated. He may see himself as a Western version of Vladimir Putin, but we don't. We see Trump as just a bully accustomed to stiffing banks (Vermonters make their payments), cheating his subcontractors (we pay them, because we're related to most of them), and treating women poorly (we just know better). Vermonters gave refuge to the Soviet dissident and Nobel Prize winner Alexandr Soltzhenitsyn; Trump is apparently ready to put our entire country in Russia's hands as Putin plays Trump's ego like Yo-Yo Ma plays a Stradivarius. The result is that the world's democracies are no longer looking to the United States for global leadership, a shocking abdication already underway due to Trump's refusal to protect the American people from foreign enemies.

Jeff and I made a good start on the book with some lists, quizzes, cartoons, and a cover. Vermonters fight back—always have and always will. And so we began this thump to The Trump.

However, we soon realized that our task was too great and the enemy too fearsome for us to do it alone. As in most hostage situations—and this was the biggest one yet in the nation's history—we needed backup. We went looking for wise, witty, and like-minded friends to make up a posse of Vermont writers and artists. In a month, we had signed up almost a score of people with kindred, righteous anger. Our duet became a chorus.

Hallelujah!

Trump Imitates Coolidge

Calvin Coolidge, the thirtieth president and the second from Vermont, was notable for the brevity and dryness of his speech. On occasion, however, he could be eloquent, as he was at Bennington in September, 1928, when he toured the state to assess recovery from the Great Flood of 1927. In part, he said:

🌿

... VERMONT IS A STATE I LOVE. I could not look upon the peaks of Ascutney, Killington, Mansfield, and Equinox, without being moved in a way that no other scene could move me. It was here that I first saw the light of day, here I received my bride, here my dead lie pillowed on the loving breast of our eternal hills.

I love Vermont because of her hills and valleys, her scenery and invigorating climate, but most of all because of her indomitable people. They are a race of pioneers who have almost beggared themselves to serve others. If the spirit of liberty should vanish in other parts of the Union, and support of our institutions should languish, it could all be replenished from the generous store held by the people of this brave little state of Vermont.[1]

Imagine if Donald Trump were governor . . .
Vermont is a state that loves ME—lots! The peaks of Ascutney, Killington, Mansfield, and Camel's Hump could not look upon me without being moved in a way that no other person could move them. And, by God, they would move to be closer to me.

---

[1] See: https://coolidgefoundation.org/resources/
speeches-as-president-1923-1929-21/.

It was here that the light of day first shone on me. Vermont's hills and valleys, her scenery and invigorating climate all love me but, for reasons that escape me, her indomitable people do not. They are a race of pioneers who have almost beggared themselves to serve others—the fools! When the spirit of liberty vanishes in other parts of the Union, I won't lift a pinkie to replenish it from the generous store in this tiny blue state. (There's no Ivanka line of clothing in that store, anyway.) No, I'll do my best to crush these upstarts who practice democracy on a human scale. Let them stew in their own sap!

Foreword:
Here's What
the Hell We Do Now

STEPHEN C. TERRY

❧

PRESIDENT TRUMP's first 100 days were bad enough—just a taste of the destructive chaos and potential calamities ahead for the next many hundreds of days. The crucial question facing Vermonters and the world is: How do we survive the remainder of the Trump presidency?

Clearly, this is not a particularly humorous matter, as the stakes are so high. If we let down our guard, we will get rolled over by the misguided Republican machine that is now running Washington.

Trump's June decision that the United States will withdraw from the 2015 Paris climate agreement was an unconscionable betrayal and abdication of American moral leadership. It told the world that the U.S. cannot be counted on to lead and join more than 190 other nations to protect the environmental health of the planet. Appalling.

For Vermont, the failure to reduce Earth's warming will result in long-term harm to the state as we know it. What will Vermont be like as a place with no maple trees, no ski industry, no dramatic change of seasons? Vermont's weather, never predictable, will likely become even more turbulent and destructive. All because President Trump has decided to use his vast power to double down and pander to his hard-core right-wing minority base while giving the rest of the country and other world leaders a middle-finger salute.

The other Trump hammer blow came in late May, as his administration released a proposed 2018 budget that was immediately attacked across the political spectrum as immoral and very detrimental to Vermont.

Here's how Trump's programs will hurt Vermont:

If the Trump-Ryan bill to repeal and replace the Obama Affordable Care Act, which passed the U.S. House by a few votes, or Trump's budget proposals are ever enacted into law, Vermont could face an estimated $200 million annual loss in federal money for health care, primarily in Medicaid support. How would we fill the hole? Do we kick people out of nursing homes?

Vermont's secretary of human services, Al Gobeille, a Republican businessman, said that Trump's proposed budget was very devastating and destructive to the people his agency serves. The budget seeks to eliminate the Low-Income Home Energy Assistance, which some 21,000 Vermont families rely on for help in meeting winter heating bills. Gobeille said this assistance is real, and without it Vermonters will freeze. Do we, as a humane state, allow them to freeze?

If Trump's Environmental Protection Agency budget is ever enacted, Vermont's efforts to achieve clean water and clean air will falter, renewable energy research may disappear, and millions of federal support dollars for the Agency of Natural Resources will be greatly reduced, if not eliminated. Do we live with more pollution? How do we reach our state goal of 90 percent renewable fuels by 2050?

The key to understanding why small rural Vermont is a large moral force for resisting Trump is rooted in our Town Meeting culture, which has long taught citizens to stand up and speak their minds. We know how to disagree—with civility, with integrity, and with compassion for differing points of view. These skills will help us resist and survive Trump. It will show the world that a rural state that did not support Trump can be a beacon of hope.

The first 100 days of Trump were filled with so many threats, from repeal of the Affordable Care Act to executive orders that would have turned our local and state police forces into a federal militia to round up undocumented dairy workers. "Feds Could ICE-Out Dairy Economy" and "Deporting Workers Would Devastate Farms" were the prophetic headlines in the *Addison Independent* newspaper, warning us of impending economic disaster.

"So far," as an old Vermonter would say, we have avoided a big hit to the farm economy, thanks to incompetent warring factions inside the White House, a dysfunctional Republican majority in Congress, a brave federal judicial system striking down Trump's immigration orders, and a revival of aggressive journalism exercising First Amendment rights.

In hindsight, the budgetary shot across Vermont's bow served as a welcome forewarning to move us to a war footing. We need to be better prepared to resist Trump's onslaught, fortified with the lessons learned from our state's history, with civic engagement, and with massive protests on steroids.

Vermonters leaders can show the other forty-nine states how one small state can and will resist. We will persist with conviction against any federal intrusion of power that would forever adversely change Vermont.

History is on our side. "This brave little state of Vermont," as President Calvin Coolidge said in Bennington in 1928, "will rally to replenish the spirit of liberty" because of its "indomitable people."

Vermont is a deep blue state, as 178,573 Hillary Clinton supporters, along with 18,218 Bernie Sanders write-ins, voted against Trump. The Manhattan real estate mogul received only 95,369 votes in November, reaffirming our blue political status.

Our very liberal Democratic three-person congressional delegation is a solid wall of opposition to Trump policies, especially his withdrawal from the Paris climate agreement. This is the type of wall we need and support. Senators Patrick Leahy and Bernie Sanders, along with Representative Peter Welch, are carrying the torches of Trump opposition for Vermonters.

Leahy, Sanders, and Welch are gearing up for a protracted battle to make sure Trump's 2018 budget, called "A New Foundation for American Greatness," is relegated to the congressional dustbin. Our three-person delegation's efforts have never been more critical. They need and deserve our support.

That said, our newly elected moderate Republican Vermont governor, Phil Scott, is one of the most popular governors in the nation, and to date the only Republican governor who has consistently opposed Donald Trump.

Within two hours after Trump withdrew from the Paris climate accord, Scott issued a statement expressing his disappointment. "Vermont has taken a leadership role in addressing climate change, and the president's decision today only strengthens our commitment," Scott said. As a result, Vermont will join other states, cities, and businesses, along with world leaders, to continue our work on meeting Paris targets for a cleaner planet. As German chancellor Angela Merkel said so eloquently, Trump's decision "will not deter all of us who feel obliged to protect this Earth."

The former New York City mayor, billionaire Michael Bloomberg, has said he will put up $15 million to continue the work of the United Nations Framework Convention on Climate Change (UNFCCC) as agreed to in Paris. "Americans are not walking away from the Paris Climate Agreement. Just the opposite—we are forging ahead," Bloomberg pledged.

Vermonters of all political persuasions have long answered the call to duty in public service, whether in defense of our national security in wartime, in response to natural or economic disasters, or to political crises that threaten our well-being. During the New Deal, Republican governor George D. Aiken led a pitchfork-armed battle against the Roosevelt Administration's plan to move people off hillside farms because these lands were deemed "sub-marginal." Aiken won. And of course, Aiken's role in the U.S. Senate opposing the Vietnam War is legendary.

Republican governor Ernest Gibson took on the business and utility establishment to propose creation of a state-owned Vermont Power Authority. This led to the formation of the Vermont Electric Power Company, the first transmission company in the nation jointly owned by in-state municipal, cooperative, and investor utilities.

In 1963, Philip H. Hoff became the first Democratic governor of Vermont in 109 years. A political revolution followed Hoff's three terms as red turned to blue in the Green Mountain State, and Vermont was changed forever. Hoff led reforms to the state education system, the judicial structure, and social welfare programs, and he inaugurated state planning, to name just a few of his many accomplishments.

Republican governor Deane C. Davis fought off the developers and his natural business allies to create Act 250, which for almost fifty years now has been the template for modern Vermont land policy.

Democratic governor Thomas P. Salmon put the brakes on development when he decreed that "Vermont is not for sale" and instituted a land-gains tax to stop short-term speculation.

Democratic governor Madeleine M. Kunin led efforts to provide more opportunities for women to serve in state government while encouraging women to run for political office at the state and local level. Mrs. Kunin continues as a leader in Vermont to get more women to hold elective office through Emerge Vermont, a campaign to encourage women to become political candidates. Currently women hold 37 percent of the 30 Vermont Senate seats, and 41 percent of the 150 Vermont House seats, including the Speaker of the House. Vermont still lags in the number of statewide elective holders, with only one female holding one of the nine statewide offices that include our Congressional Delegation, which continues to be an all-male preserve.

Republican governor Richard A. Snelling started his own version of an FDR-type New Deal program to create public-works jobs to help pull the state out of a deep economic recession.

In 2000, Democratic governor Howard Dean signed the Civil Unions Law, making Vermont the first state in the nation to adopt civil unions for gay couples. This led, after Dean left office, to Vermont becoming the first state to allow same-sex marriage through legislative action instead of by a court ruling.

In 2001, Republican U.S. Senator Jim Jeffords took the extraordinary and principled step of leaving his lifelong party to become an independent, shifting control of the U.S. Senate to the Democratic Party. Jeffords said that he didn't leave the Republican Party, but that the party left him.

Republican governor Jim Douglas led reform of the state health care system with the Blueprint for Health, a forerunner of the Obama Affordable Care Act.

Democratic governor Peter Shumlin shouldered the political risk of advocating single-payer health care for all Vermonters, and he took the unprecedented step of focusing his second State of the State address on the need to combat opiate addiction, a model effort that is now being followed nationwide.

Republican governor Phil Scott recently joined Democrats and Progressives in the state legislature to build a legal wall shielding most undocumented workers, especially those in the dairy industry, from unchecked federal immigration arrests.

When the reality sank in that Trump was actually going to be the forty-fifth president of the United States, Vermonters began immediately planning for the battle ahead to keep Vermont the Last Great Place. The day after the presidential inauguration, thousands of Vermonters marched in Montpelier as well as Washington, DC, joining hundreds of thousands of their brethren throughout the entire United States and the world to show their determination to fight and to resist. This resistance will continue, and its numbers will swell: voices from the grassroots will not be stilled.

Independent Bernie Sanders began a political revolution in Burlington in the 1980s. Today he is America's most popular U.S. Senator and is tirelessly battling Trump and his plutocracy. As Bernie reminds us, "enough is enough."

That, President Trump, is no Vermont joke or fake news!

The Full Vermonty

Vermont in the Age of Trump

The Truth Can Hurt

Bernard DeVoto

The historian and writer Bernard DeVoto won both a Pulitzer Prize and the National Book Award late in his career. In the mid-1930s, he traveled through Vermont and wrote an incisive article, "How to Live among the Vermonters." DeVoto described how, in the 1920s, as young people had left Vermont, older people had come, mostly as summer folk. DeVoto took note of their acculturation and concluded with an anecdote for our times.

❧

. . . A GOOD MANY OF THESE PEOPLE think of themselves as citizens of Vermont and all of them are intensely local in their pride of place. The taxes they pay are vital to the towns, and their summer expenditures help to make the economic life of Vermont stable. But all of them must serve an apprenticeship before they get their paper. They need time to learn how to get along with the people to whose country they have immigrated. Time and much remembering and forgetting—in order to recover an American way of life so nearly vanished in other sections that the effort to return to it must be almost archeological.

A rich folklore could be drawn on for illustration. Let one story suffice; it is one which Robert Frost attributed to Walter Hard. You are to picture the usual group at evening on the porch of the general store, and talk has grown nostalgic about the old-time education, when you studied under the invitation of the whip and book-learning was larruped into you to stay. It is agreed that that was the soundest technic of instruction and that in those days what a man learned counted for something. But one is a protestant. His dissent is packed with a feeling for the irremediable injustice of this world, the evil and frustrations that are integral in human life. With the helplessness of mortality to avert the injuries inflicted on its innocence, he says, "The only time I was ever licked, 'twas for telling the truth." Silence while his neighbors receive this fact, examine it, and check it against the teachings of experience. Then, quietly, judicially, with an air of rendering exact justice in the light of eternal truths, one says, "Well, Sam, it cured ye!"

Bernard DeVoto, "How to Live among the Vermonters," *Harper's Magazine*, vol. 73 (August 1936), pp. 333–36.

Vermont Will Stump
the Trump

BOB STANNARD

WELL DONE, AMERICA. This is a fine mess you've gotten us into. Thanks to an antiquated electoral college—a system designed to keep us from electing a narcissistic, misogynistic, corrupt, golfing goofball with bad hair—a minority of voters have succeeded in electing a narcissistic, misogynistic, corrupt, golfing goofball with bad hair. Most Americans are now freaking out over the colossal error they have just made . . . but not Vermonters.

Vermonters have been around for a long time. We survived the Revolution, an attempted takeover by New York (though we still allow some of them to come back here for a visit), winter, black flies, Volvos, a recession and its recovery (see my TWO books on the subject), the reclassification of our maple syrup, and bad crops. Surviving an idiot president with bad hair will have no more influence on the average Vermonter than having the back buckle on his suspenders give out (why do you think we wear a belt with our suspenders?).

Vermonters were born ready for anything. There is no calamity too big that would cause a Vermonter to get all jacked up and to spit from his wad of chew, secured firmly in between his teeth and right cheek, onto your shoe. Okay, perhaps if the

DRIVING A SNO-CAT

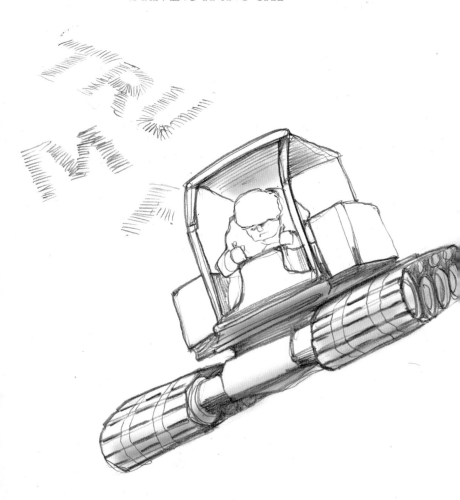

orange-haired buffoon were to get into a nuclear shoot-out with the other idiot world leader from North Korea with equally as bad hair, that might get our attention. Then again, if the fish are biting it might take a week to ten days for us to notice.

Unlike the rest of you stressed-out, overworked helicopter parents out there, who fret over every little thing including the smudge on little Johnny's shirt, Vermonters tend to not mind smudges. Are we at all concerned that we have a president who doesn't believe in science, has no clue what he's doing, is more focused on winning than getting it right, and surrounds himself with people even more clueless than he is? Well, sure. We're not idiots, but we know how to survive idiots. Like I said, we've been doing so for roughly 250 years; we can wade through another four.

So just how do we cope with what will arguably go down as the worst presidency in American history? First, we can stop and marvel at the good fortune that will be bestowed on George W. Bush. No one in Vermont ever thought he'd *ever* shed the mantel of being the worst president ever; nevertheless, he's already done this in less than eight months—four months, even!

We'll do what Vermonters have always done. We'll hang around our diners and country stores and gab away about Trump's latest stupid thing, like sending an aircraft carrier in the wrong direction (I mean who hasn't made that mistake at least once in their life?). We'll spend some time jawbonin' and cipherin' as to how we'd do whatever Trump's doing but do it differently. We'll argue about whose idea is the best (of course it would be mine, as your ideas are always stupid), and in the end we'll just go on about our business.

Yup, so while the rest of you are wringing your hands, tearing what little hair you have left out by the roots, and packing to move to Canada (it's freakin' cold there, ya know), you can all rest assured that Vermont and Vermonters will be just fine. In the words of the chair of the selectboard of one of the towns I represented when I was in the legislature, in response to a discussion about having the state of Vermont come into town and declare how things are going to be, he said, "You send them boys right on down here and we'll blow their freakin' heads right off."

Thus, in a nutshell, Vermonters are a peaceful lot—so long as you don't mess with our maple syrup and the rest of our way of life. Just chill. Trump will be gone before the next cutting of hay.

The Ghost of John Dewey

MICHAEL S. MARTIN

❧

JOHN DEWEY'S GRAVE WAS A MESS. Hosta plants had been blasted out of the earth, lilac branches snapped, grass seared, the gravestone scorched, as if some supernatural force had erupted beneath his final resting place in his native Vermont soil. A groundskeeper had found the strange scene in the spring of Donald Trump's presidency, but few people thought much of it. After all, Vermonters tend to not get carried away and they don't spook easily. As a rule, they stubbornly adhere to facts and common sense, and don't go in for fearmongering, hoodoo, and bogeymen.

It was only later that folks realized that the Trump presidency had literally turned John Dewey over in his grave. Only something as foul, strange, and unnatural as the Trump Administration could have stirred the Burlington-born social philosopher to return from the great beyond. After devoting ninety years of his life to defending democracy and progressive ideas, writing books such as *Ethics*, *Democracy and Education*, and *Freedom and Culture*, Dewey's spirit must have been reluctant to rise from its repose to once again remind Americans of some plain truths. The same way a Vermonter quietly curses and stoically puts snow boots back on before shoveling the driveway after repeated nor'easters, Dewey's ghost must have mumbled a

"Byjezuss!" and emerged from Vermont's rock ribs to pull our country back from the brink of total nonsense, or worse.

After the shock of the election had worn off, most Vermonters moved morosely through the phases of grief—but sometimes acceptance is hard. And as the Trump White House sank to lower depths of nepotism, corruption, mendacity, and comic incompetence, Dewey's ghost must have found it plain unacceptable, and decided, reluctantly, to walk among us once again to remind us of what democracy is, before it was too late.

It's believed that Moustafa actually saw the restless spirit of Dewey first, just after a noontime lecture at UVM, not far from his upturned grave near Ira Allen Chapel. George was selling goat cheese at the farmer's market when he saw the specter. Charlie was driving the kids home from soccer practice when he saw Dewey's ghost in the crosswalk, just as plain as day. Judy was on her rider mower with headphones on when, at dusk, she spotted Dewey's ghost at the edge of her yard.

However, Vermonters are an ungovernable lot, so naturally people disagreed about exactly which John Dewey had returned. Some saw the fiery young philosopher of *The School and Society* in his doctoral robes, with a broad bushy mustache and eyes full of ardor. Others said he had appeared to them as the bespectacled smiling saint of *Knowing and the Known*, around the time that Dwight Eisenhower had called Dewey the "Philosopher of Freedom." Still others had recognized a middle-aged Dewey, cropped salt-and-pepper mustache, white hair, and dark suit, just as he appeared when he was living and working in China and Japan.

Americans tend to blame all of society's ills on public schools, and the election of Donald J. Trump was no exception. People asked, what the hell were they teaching kids that we could have elected such a buffoon to the White House? Whatever happened to an educated citizenry? Why couldn't the Millennials throw Hillary a vote after their love affair with Bernie? Didn't schools teach civics anymore?

As a former classroom teacher, principal, and professor, Dewey's ghost probably felt obligated to defend the great American institution of public schooling. After all, it was Dewey who wrote: *Education is the fundamental method of progress and reform.* Even if it meant leaving the afterlife for a while, there's no way that America's greatest pedagogue could find eternal rest while Betsy DeVos sold out public schools to ravenous for-profit charters and religious extremists. Back in the 1930s, Dewey had warned against the "business mind" becoming even more powerful than government, and clearly the Trump Inc. presidency now tormented his spirit.

Trump's proposed cuts to funding the arts must have pained Dewey's soul as well. For Dewey, the arts were an essential ingredient of a democratic society. *Art is the most effective mode of communication that exists,* he wrote.

Trump's travel bans and race baiting likely burned up Dewey's ashes too. Systematic hatred of any human group—racial, sectarian, political—denotes deep-seated skepticism about the qualities of human nature, Dewey believed.

So while President Trump tweeted monosyllabic blasts of "BAD!," "SAD!," "LOSER!," and "NUTJOB!," John Dewey's ghost went to work. In a sort of anti-Twitter campaign, it provided Vermonters with complete sentences and cogent ideas. The ghost whispered on the wind fully developed thoughts such as: *There cannot be two sets of ethical principles, one for life in the school, and the other for life outside the school,* and solid reasoning such as: *I don't believe people learn merely by doing. The important things are the ideas a man puts into his doing.*

Suddenly people found key passages from Dewey on their

tablets, e-readers, and web pages for example: *We have advanced far enough to say that democracy is a way of life. We have yet to realize that it is a way of personal life and one which provides a moral standard for personal conduct.*

In homes, books mysteriously fell off shelves and opened to selections such as: *There is no physical acid which has the corrosive power possessed by intolerance directed against persons because they belong to a group that bears a certain name. Its corrosive power gains with what it feeds on.*

In libraries, dusty editions of Dewey were found open to excerpts such as: *When we allow ourselves to be fear-ridden and permit it to dictate how we act, it is because we have lost faith in our fellow countrymen—and that is the unforgivable sin against the spirit of democracy.*

Teachers started to rediscover the democratic mission of schools. In Randolph, there was a symposium on what it means to be socially engaged. In Rutland, they put on a global-issues conference and invited teachers and students from other schools. In Burlington, the International Club created a graphic with a dove and open hands to spread a message of peace and inclusion. It went viral immediately.

Gradually, parents started treating teachers with a little more respect, deference even. They were grateful that their children were learning about timely topics such as checks and balances, constitutional crises, special counsels, foreign-agent registration, subpoenas, conflicts of interest, impeachment, and the role of a free press in a democracy. Civics became cool again. Social consciousness was in vogue for domestic issues. Critical thinking became indispensable for dealing with fake news, Orwellian press briefings, and presidential riffs and rambles. Younger students played at finding the spelling, geography, and history errors in the president's tweets and speeches. It was fun to go to school again.

In the end, the teachers' unions decided to send President Trump a thank-you card. After all, he had made their work relevant again and reminded Americans of some very important civics lessons.

Somewhere, the spirit of America's favorite teacher, John Dewey, was smiling. Democracy would endure. The kids were all right. He could finally get some rest.

"Who's Afraid of the Big Bad Wolf?"

❧

In these fraught times, we have a great challenge educating the young about the world around them, to recognize truth from falsehood, science from pseudo-science, real news from fake news. Through stories, they can learn about the heroism, cleverness and strength needed to confront the evil before their eyes. The following stories are also aptly suited to the educational mission described in Mike Martin's essay.

Where the Wild Things Are

Pinocchio

Chicken Little

Robin Hood

How the Elephant Got His Trump

Goodnight, Doofus!

Cloudy and 100 Percent Chance of Meatheads!

Lyddie

A Is for Activists

How the Grinch Stole Christmas

Oh, the Things you can Think, When *You Think!*

Curious George and Uncurious Donald

Escape Literature

Bill Mares

You can't be thinking about Trump all the time. You need a respite. Why not turn off all your screens and pull out your ear buds, and read a good book or poem? Vermont authors have written many. Here are a few . . .

Tom Bassett, *Outsiders Inside Vermont*

Chris Bohjalian, *Midwives*

Frank Bryan, *Real Democracy*

Frank Bryan and Bill Mares, *Real Vermonters Don't Milk Goats*

Jeff Danziger, *Conscience of a Cartoonist*

Deane C. Davis, *Justice in the Mountain*

Allen Foley, *What the Old-Timer Said*

Robert Frost, *Collected Poems*—especially "Mending Wall"[2] and "New Hampshire"[3]

Gerald Jay Goldberg, *The Lynching of Owen Newfield*

2 Includes the line "Something there is that doesn't love a wall."
3 The last of 413 lines in this poem reads: "At present I am living in Vermont."

Sam Hand, Tony Marro, and Steve Terry, *Philip Hoff*

Edward Hoagland, *The Courage of Turtles*

Jim Jeffords, *My Declaration of Independence*

Galway Kinnell, *The Book of Nightmares*

Madeleine Kunin, *Living a Political Life*

Jeffrey Lent, *In the Fall*

Sinclair Lewis, *It Can't Happen Here*

Stephen Martin, *Orville's Revenge: The Anatomy of a Suicide*

Archer Mayor, *any* of his Brattleboro mysteries

Peter Miller, *Deer Camp*

Howard Mosher, *Disappearances*—or any of his other books

Jernigan Pontiac, *Hackie*

Bill Schubart, *The Lamoille Stories*

Bob Stannard, *How to Survive the Recession*

Subversion, Not Resistance, in the Age of donald j

CHRISTOPHER LOURAS

❧

AS MANY VERMONTERS FEEL we are in the rear row of a beat-up and weathered Econoline van careening down Route 100 toward an uncertain future in the age of donald j, we wonder aloud who holds the wheel and how the ride ends.

In our town halls, in our hockey rinks, in our diners, and at our kitchen tables, the telling of mistruths and general incivility have been normalized. We seek validation not only from like-minded people but in unlikely places as we find families divided and friendships strained. (I found myself asking my bride of twenty-one years: "Will you admit you miss Bush if I admit I miss Obama?" We both decided "Yup.")

But simply commiserating accomplishes little. Some of us need a plan, a strategy, to endure the daily mindscrew borne of each successive tweet or executive order. How do we solve a problem like donald j? The answer: We Don't. Focusing solely on "45" and his actions is indeed a fool's errand. In eighty years, history will look back and not judge the tiny-fisted troll currently occupying the White House, but *will* judge those who put him there and those who did nothing once he arrived.

In that spirit, I offer the following opportunities for current leaders, future leaders, and community members.

In an administration hobbled by incompetency and inaction (whether by design or simply fortuitous happenstance), an inescapable void will result. Into this void governors and mayors must step. Policies curtailed or ignored must be resurrected by state and local officials, and the corresponding shift in power will leave a correspondingly ineffectual and understaffed federal government ill-equipped to challenge the emerging power structure. Out of today's chaos we likely will see a weakening of federal primacy and a corresponding renewal of states' rights and local control. Indeed, we are currently witnessing the evolution of this new dynamic as governors nationwide, including our own Phil Scott, join the Climate Alliance to uphold the principles of the Paris Accord. Likewise, mayors have taken up the climate mantle, and, with governors, they most assuredly must pursue other initiatives ignored by the Feds, such as water-quality standards, police reform, and immigration reform.

Beyond state and local officials seizing power and exercising authority, we must also encourage our next generation to prepare to transform our nation and world. While some of us languish with a sense of foreboding, others see opportunity. For our youth, the age of donald j can be a strange and awe-inspiring time to be alive, to learn, and to ready themselves to take the reins. As the current administration continues to assail our institutions (e.g., the "political establishment," the media, the arts), academia will become a bastion where our future leaders can question, learn, and gain the critical-thinking skills required to recover from and repair what may be wrought over the next four years. As with the post-World War Two generation, the young men and women who choose to serve our nation whether in military or civilian work, will find themselves uniquely prepared to lead, building on those critical character traits developed during their public service: empathy, initiative, and integrity.

Finally, and perhaps most importantly, we must hold ourselves accountable in our own communities. There are those of us who avoid conflict, while others revel in it. Those, like donald j, who create chaos and who traffic in false narratives must not be allowed to go unchallenged. Though uncomfortable, we must call out and push back against those neighbors who seek to demean and deface our culture and our society by emulating the behaviors modeled by the president. While we will undoubtedly be judged by history, we must also take personal measure of ourselves as we look in the mirror each morning.

SPLITTING WOOD

WHERE'S THE MEXICAN KID
THAT GOES ON THE END
OF THIS THING?

"Freedom and Unity" Still Speaks—Against Trump!

Tom Slayton

❧

How should Vermonters respond to Donald Trump's presidency? By being Vermonters—independent, feisty, and unafraid to speak truth to power. And to stupidity!

One example of this state's determined opposition to just about everything Trump stands for was the huge, spontaneous women's pink-cap demonstration that shut down Montpelier in late January 2017. It was the largest demonstration in Montpelier's history: an estimated 20,000 Vermonters surged over the State House lawn and all the way across State Street and up the facing steps of the State Office Building. The crowd was orderly, but it was so large that Montpelier police declared the city closed for the day. Cars attempting to get into town were turned away and were backed up for five miles along Interstate 89.

Despite the chilly day and the grim prospect of a Trump presidency, the mood of the crowd was not glum. If there is such a thing as cheerful anger—determined, happy outrage—that was the tone of the huge gathering. It was, in effect, a giant third finger raised joyfully toward Washington.

"Science is Real!" said one of the thousands of signs. "I will not go quietly back to the 1950s," said another. "Yuge Mistake!"

and "Love Trumps Hate" were favorites. Perhaps the funniest was a picture of the new president with the words: "Does This ASS make my country look Small?"

Another form of opposition—smaller, quieter, but just as heartfelt and just as typical of Vermont's opposition to our current president's bigotry and mendacity—had occurred a few weeks earlier, after Trump's election but before his inauguration. A piece of hate mail echoing Trump's anti-Muslim statements had been sent to the Islamic Society of Vermont in Colchester. The response of the state's religious communities was swift and positive. Vermont Interfaith Action, an ecumenical social justice group with members from religious organizations across the state, organized a prayer service with the Muslim group. More than 100 Vermonters of various faiths came to the Islamic Society's Colchester center and joined the 100 Muslims assembled there to show their support. A few members of the group said supportive words and the Reverend Mara Dowdall of the Burlington Unitarian-Universalist Church brought a box of cards from its Sunday School children expressing love and support. But, basically, Interfaith Action members didn't actually do anything except the most important thing: they showed up and stood shoulder to shoulder with their neighbors. It was simply a demonstration of common decency—of community. If the big women's demonstration was a symbolic third finger, this smaller, quieter action was, in its own way, just as effective, an unmistakeable STOP sign directed at Washington.

The two actions could be seen as a restatement of the Vermont motto: "Freedom and Unity." That motto summarizes both the longtime Vermont love of individual freedom and the state's concomitant affection for and devotion to community life. The big demo was an unmistakable show of Vermonters' right to free expression and their resistance to any efforts, however crude, to suppress it. And the show of support for the Islamic Society congregation was a spontaneous expression of our determination to stand by all members of the community, no exclusions.

Vermonters still treasure both freedom and unity. And as long as we are unafraid to speak out, our state will remain a rock of opposition to the creepy clown in the White House.

Latinos in Vermont before, during, and (con esperanza) after the Trump Years

Julia Alvarez

❧

WHEN I MOVED TO VERMONT IN 1988, my Latino friends wondered how I was going to survive up in *el norte* of El Norte. Wasn't it one of the whitest states in the United States? (Second, after Maine.) And what about *el frío*? Half a year of cold weather! (Anything below fifty degrees, they considered *frío*.) Was I crazy *loca*? (Repeating the word in both languages intensified my craziness.)

After a winter in Vermont, I recounted how the people were so warmhearted that *el frío* didn't seem so cold. Neighbors helped me shovel my walk, haul my car out of a snowdrift. They brought me eggs from their chicken houses (I had no idea hens lay eggs in cold weather!), and syrup from their sugar-bush once the days started to warm up and the sap to run. My Vermont farm community actually reminded me of my native Dominican Republic: both agrarian cultures, following those elemental rhythms of the seasons, the planting and harvesting of crops, the care of animals, and of each other. Neighborliness was essential for survival: whether it was a hurricane or a blizzard, a drought or a flood, or the dozen daily needs that come up, we needed each other.

But there was no getting around the issue of diversity. "Not many brown faces here," my Latino friends noted when they came to visit. They were right. It was rare to meet another Hispanic/Latino, much less a Dominican. The census of 1990 in Vermont didn't even report a Hispanic population—not enough of us around to count. It was a progressive state in many ways: a strong activist presence from the many former anti-war, anti-establishment, back-to-the-land young people who settled here in the 1960s and 1970s; leadership in environmental issues and in gay rights (we were the state where 350.org was founded, and one of the first states to allow civil unions and gay marriages); annual peace festivals and concerts, attended by thousands; our biggest city, Burlington, had the only socialist mayor in the whole country, Bernie Sanders. "*El es de Nueva York*," I boasted for Brown points to my Latino friends back in Queens and *el Bronx*.

I settled down in my *querido* Vermont, not for the max two years my friends had predicted, but now going on twenty-nine years. I married the local ophthalmologist (who had done mission trips in my native country—how endearing is that?!). We formed our own melded family, which resembled the eclectic, complicated extended *familia* I grew up in. At Middlebury College, where I taught all those years until my retirement in 2016, a generous influx of Latinos during the summer language schools and of Latino faculty and students during the regular sessions gave me a skewed sense that there was *some* Latino diversity in my adopted state. Still, every few months I found myself needing to go back to the DR, or at the very least, Nueva York, to get (what I called) a shot of the homeland. In fact, my Nebraskan-born husband Bill and I ended up becoming involved in a long-distance coffee farm and literacy project in my native land. There, I got the much-needed periodic doses of Spanish, Dominican culture, food, and daily infusions from the coffee we grew, which we also brought back to Vermont.

But it was always either/or: my all-American life or *mi vida Dominicana*. How long could I keep up such an internal tug of war? So I was thrilled to learn from Chris Rimmer of VINS (now Vermont Eco-Studies) about the Bicknell's thrush, which summers in our Green Mountains of Vermont and winters on the very mountains where our farm is located in the Dominican Republic. If a little bird could do it, so could I.

Then, about fifteen years ago, something odd started happening. I began getting calls from local schools and from the very same neighbors who had helped me out of snowdrifts and kept me in fresh eggs asking if I could come over and translate for a monolingual Spanish-speaking student or worker on their crew. My husband reported that farmers were bringing Mexican migrant workers to his office with eye problems. It turned out that more and more of our ailing dairy farms were hiring undocumented workers from my part of the world, willing to work for lower wages around the clock and the calendar in order to send back remittances to their families who could no longer survive by farming back home. Without their affordable help, my farmer neighbors would not be able to keep on farming, either. As many as 500 "undercover" Latinos were now a mostly invisible part of my county!

The Latino-ization of Vermont had begun! We began showing up in the state census. In the course of my twenty-nine years here, Latinos have become the state's largest minority group, rising from 5,504 in the 2000 census to 10,226 today—that's only

1.6 percent of our state's population, compared to 16.9 percent nationally. But change is often slow, and it doesn't always happen during our watch. Still, I've lived to see Latinos become a real, if small, presence in Vermont. And with that presence have come social services, advocacy groups, clinics, and other organized ways of unfolding the welcome mat.

But for a while, before these services and groups of volunteers caught up with this new demographic, a few of us Spanish speakers were often called on—our phone numbers passed around the Mexican migrant community—whenever there was a need: someone was ill and needed to be driven to the doctor; a little Mexican girl had shown up at a local elementary school and needed a tutor; a teenage mother was giving birth at the hospital and needed help understanding instructions (¡Empuja! Push! ¡Respira! Breathe!) as well as some homegrown comfort. Then the more pedestrian daily and weekly needs: trips to grocery stores, to churches, to Western Union counters to send money home. Occasionally, I drove someone to the airport for the flight to Mexico for a sad or happy event—a funeral or a child's birth—or just for that shot of the homeland, a need I understood all too well.

When I asked my new *amigos* the same question I had been asked—Why had they come to a cold place like Vermont?—many gave the same answers I had given my friends: Vermont was a good place to work, mostly decent *patrones*, consistent employment, as much work as they wanted, kind people, the peacefulness of an agrarian life. "*Muy tranquilo,*" they often said. A tranquil place. There were seldom raids by *la Migra* (Immigration and Customs Enforcement—ICE). They felt safe.

I was proud of our state for its welcome and socially just response to a population it recognized as necessary for its own survival. Vermont became one of the few states to allow undocumented persons to obtain a driver's license, to refuse to use our law-enforcement officers as agents for ICE, to enact a statewide Fair and Impartial Policing Policy forbidding the targeting or detaining of people for noncriminal infractions. Four Vermont cities, among them my own hometown, Middlebury, have begun the process of becoming sanctuary cities.

Of course, Vermont is home to a population of diverse political beliefs and points of view. Not every Vermonter wanted these "aliens" and "illegals" here. Not every law-enforcement officer stayed within the confines mandated by our state. There were raids, arrests, deportations, even, sadly, a death: twenty-year-old José Cruz died as a result of a farm accident—*que en paz descanse.* But with every crisis came a corresponding surge of solidarity: advocates stepping forward, visiting jails, collecting donations, donating professional services, accompanying José's body home.

But after the election of Trump and the many threats of deportations, the insulting rhetoric hurled at those from our part of the world, and the threats of economic repercussions to states and communities that chose to defy the government and become sanctuary cities, my pride in my country, if not my state, is increasingly eroding. Often, I find myself apologizing to workers I've gotten to know as friends, to their kids I've mentored who are now in high school and on their way to college, to my neighbors who are worried about what will happen to their dairy farms if they lose the backbone of their workforce.

After the Trump election I've been watching the news, including footage of families crossing our Vermont border into Canada. Will our Vermont Latino population decrease, and again become so small that it won't even register in the next census? Was the word already spreading that our state is no longer a safe place to work in? I've played and replayed the news clips of the families leaving, anticipating crackdowns, dragging their wheeled suitcases on the snowy ground into Canada. They keep their heads bowed and their faces averted, as if they are the ones who should be ashamed of what this country of immigrants had forgotten about its origins and its commitment to welcome all those pursuing life, liberty, and the pursuit of happiness.

❧

*For more specific suggestions on how to be the change you want to
see happen in our state and beyond, consider donating or volun-
teering with local organizations providing services and advocacy to
our migrant worker population, including:*

Migrant Justice, https://migrantjustice.net/

American Civil Liberties Union of Vermont, https://www.
acluvt.org/

Local churches and community groups

Judith Levine's piece in *Vermont Digger,* "Eight Ways
to Defend Vermont's Undocumented Migrants," is
detailed and helpful: https://vtdigger.org/2017/03/13/
judith-levine-eight-ways-defend-vermonts-undocument-
ed-migrants/.

❧

El pueblo unido, jamás será vencido.

A united people will never be defeated.

High Noon at Highgate

BILL MARES

❧

THE FEDERAL GOVERNMENT is not the only entity that can build a wall. Fortunately, we'll only need one about forty-five miles long across the boundary with Massachusetts. In the north, we have our friends the Quebecois. On the east, we have the Connecticut River. On our west, we're guarded by Lake Champlain.

Our wall will be built with hedgerows of kale genetically modified to be eight feet tall. It will be a bipartisan effort from Republican governor Phil Scott, a contractor, and Democratic lieutenant governor David Zuckerman, an organic farmer. (Sorry, David, this GMO is for a good cause!)

Vermont will become a refuge for folks from both blue and red states, fleeing from polluted waters, fouled air, and never-ending Trump rallies. Each year we will admit a certain number of people with needed skills, giving preference to disillusioned Trump supporters. Our own EB-5 program[4] will be scandal-free.

---

4 Under this program, entrepreneurs (and their spouses and unmarried children under twenty-one) are eligible to apply for a green card (permanent residence) by making a "necessary investment in a commercial enterprise in the United States," and creating or preserving ten permanent full-time jobs for qualified U.S. workers.

For everybody else, because we don't want to be inhospitable (after all, Vermont was called "The Beckoning Country" back in the 1960s); we will invite, even encourage, them to "invest" in Vermont by buying some land. Tom Salmon, a good governor in tough times, famously said, "Vermont is not for sale." Well, we'll have to revise that for our own Time of Troubles. "Get a place in Vermont!" will be *our* slogan.

That "place" would be 100 square inches, slightly bigger than a hand- or boot-print. Thus there would be about 60,000 plots in an acre, and with 5.6 million acres in the state, we have a real land bank of some 30 billion "places" in Vermont. We could sell one to every person on earth and still have enough for ourselves.

The mind boggles at the thought of it.

QUIZ #1

Citizenship Test—At the Border

BILL MARES

1. *On one particular January 31, Ida M. Fuller of Ludlow received $22.34. Thus, she became America's first . . .* [1]
A. Lottery winner.
B. Beneficiary of a flood insurance policy.
C. Recipient of Social Security
D. Woman voter in a presidential election.

2. *Which of the following did the Vermont Legislature designate as the official State pie?*
A. Chicken pot
B. Pumpkin
C. Cow
D. Apple
E. 3.14159265358979323846264338327950288 . . .

---

1 Most of the questions in this chapter and "Facts and Alternative Facts" come from the classic *The Vermont Quiz Book* by Frank and Lee Bryan, Shelburne: New England Press, 1986

3. *In which of the following does Vermont exceed*
   New Hampshire?
   A. Population
   B. Height of its mountains
   C. Area
   D. Number of state legislators

4. *Of Vermont and New Hampshire, which state ... (circle*
   correct answer)

A. Has colder Februaries?	VT	NH
B. Voted for Roosevelt in 1936?	VT	NH
C. Has more lawyers per capita?	VT	NH
D. Is the home of *Yankee* magazine?	VT	NH

5. *Who won the American Civil War?*
   A. Grant
   B. Sherman
   C. Stannard
   D. Lincoln

6. *In which of these was Vermont NOT the first state?*
   A. First to outlaw slavery in its constitution
   B. First to institute voting exclusively by mail
   C. First to graduate an African American from college
   D. First to have a state symphony orchestra

7. *The Revolutionary War battle fought entirely in Vermont*
   was the Battle of ...
   A. Bennington.
   B. St. Albans.
   C. Caanan.
   D. Hubbardton.

8. *Which Vermont governor was born in Vermont?*
   A. Howard Dean
   B. Peter Shumlin ·
   C. Madeleine Kunin
   D. Jim Douglas
   E. Richard Snelling

9. *Roads built to bypass toll roads are called . . .*
A. "no-tolls."
B. "shunpikes."
C. "byways."
D. "roundabouts."

10. *How many gallons of maple sap are needed to make one gallon of maple syrup?*
A. 10
B. 20
C. 40
D. 75
E. 120

11. *Name the Vermont State Vegetable.*
A. Sheffield potato
B. Gilfeather turnip
C. Bennington collard greens
D. Lamoille pinto beans
E. Sharon sweet onion

12. *Pair the state and the motto:*

A. Live Free or Die	Virginia
B. *Sic Semper Tyrannis*	Mississippi
C. Liberty and Prosperity	New Hampshire
D. Freedom and Unity	Florida
E. In God We Trust	New Jersey
F. By Valor and Arms	Vermont

13. Pair the authors with their books:

A. Pearl Buck   *In the Fall*
B. William Lederer   *Understood Betsy*
C. Howard Mosher   *The Jungle Books*
D. Jeffrey Lent   *Cancer Ward*
E. Dorothy Canfield Fisher   *The Ugly American*
F. Rudyard Kipling   *The Good Earth*
G. Alexandr Solzhenitsyn   *Disappearances*

14. Justin Morgan worked in Randolph as a . . .

A. Blacksmith.
B. Schoolmaster.
C. Innkeeper.
D. Newspaper editor.
E. Farmer.

15. Circle the town/county combinations that don't fit.

A. Addison Town / Addison County
B. Chittenden Town / Chittenden County
C. Orange Town / Orange County
D. Windham Town / Windham County
E. Rutland Town / Rutland County
F. Franklin Town / Franklin County
G. Essex Town / Essex County
H. Windsor Town / Windsor County
I. Washington Town / Washington County
J. Bennington Town / Bennington County
K. Grand Isle Town / Grand Isle County
L. Orleans Town / Orleans County

Media Freak-out in East Chutney

DAVID GRAM

❧

THE EAST CHUTNEY SELECTBOARD meeting Monday night was attended by the three board members . . . Rich, Rick, and Dick Brothers, as well as Town Clerk Mary Brothers, whom everyone called Sister. The audience included Danny White, reporter for the *Daily Trumpet*, who trailed a cloud of gin fumes; two twenty-something reporters from the online news site *VTBigger*; and the ninety-four-year-old chair of the library board of trustees, Blanche Pickle.

Ms. Pickle, long known as prim and proper, was beginning to loosen up a bit, thanks to a touch of dementia. When she heard someone mention the president, she stood and said, "I would just love to give him a kiss. I don't mean on the lips, I mean on his tiny little thingy, although with my trembling hands and failing eyes I might need tweezers and a magnifying glass."

A snoozing Danny White stirred in his chair, while one of the *VTBigger* reporters jumped up, ran to her car, drove nine miles at breakneck speed to where it was rumored you could get a cell phone signal, and began tweeting furiously. Just 3.7 seconds later, this was the lead headline in the *Puffington Host*: "Vt. Nonagenarian: I'd Lewinsky Trump." The sub-headline was "Plays tiny hands meme to the max." Seconds later someone with the Twitter handle @Monicakneepads replied: "Never wanted to be a verb, but I guess there are worse things."

Trump was on the phone with Putin, seeking permission to bomb another empty Syrian airfield, but said, "Excuse me, sir, may I put you on hold? We have a domestic crisis unfolding." He then tweeted: "Fake news about fake sex," and included the new Twitter feature that plays audio as soon as someone clicks on the tweet. The song was the Marvin Gaye tune "There Ain't Nothin' Like the Real Thing, Baby." Steve Bannon then ran in and turned up the audio on the basis that Gaye's being shot dead by his father was another example of the horrible violence gripping America's hellhole inner cities. The other *VTBigger* reporter stayed behind at the selectboard meeting to shoot video of the bedlam that didn't unfold. (It consisted of Dick Brothers saying, "Yes, Blanche, okay, moving on, and Sister, could you strike that from the minutes?") It should be noted that by now, *VTBigger* employed 80 percent of the journalists in Vermont and was able to send two reporters to each legislative committee room, as well as to the 251 weekly selectboard meetings around the state. The eponymous organ had been founded eight years earlier by Sarah Bigger, a five-foot, one-inch dynamo who was just back from a twelve-minute vacation and had resumed her normal schedule of 4:00 a.m. to 2:00 a.m.

Ms. Pickle's comments got more attention nationally than in Vermont. *Breitbart*, the *National Review*, and the *Wall Street Journal* editorial page all speculated that only in a state that had offered the country Bernie Sanders could such a lewd suggestion have been made in a public forum, just another sign of liberal moral depravity. Bill O'Reilly devoted his new "Question of the Day" segment to this: "Will Ms. Pickle remove her dentures?"

The local coverage was a bit more muted. Danny White woke just in time to reconstruct events and was able to report that "Ms. Pickle made a spicy comment." That came deep in a story that led with the selectboard's debate over whether to change the town's bottled-water vendor.

The AP picked up on the story four days later, and by the following Monday's meeting, the *Washington Most* sent a reporter to gauge the aftermath. She arrived during mud season in four-inch pumps and spiked elbows, and took her seat in the front row. The selectboard had just resumed its debate on the bottled-water vendor, when, three miles down the road, a breeze blew a leaf off a tree, the leaf struck a wire owned by the regional electric cooperative, and power went out for all 211 customers in a ten-mile radius, including the East Chutney Town Hall.

By the time the power came back on, all the town's road-maintenance contracts had been awarded to a local company called Brothers Brothers Construction. No one could quite explain how this had happened, but the *Washington Most* reporter had a theory: The corruption and nepotism that had put Ivanka and Jared in charge of the country had spread even to small-town America. She decided she needed an especially pithy lede that would sum up the story and tickle her editor's fancy, and came up with this: "Democracy dies in darkness."

HELPING WITH CHORES

Jeeter von Trump

BILL SCHUBART

✿

"I T CAME. Spit-kit's here, jus' like Ross said," Jeeter von Trump shouted to himself, opening his mailbox.

Thelma, the mail delivery lady, can't see Jeeter's cellar hole from Wheelock Road, only the wooden mailbox he checks every morning after he hears Thelma's mufflerless VW bug pull away, leaving a cloud of blue smoke.

Jeeter loves the colorful flyers he gets. Not only does he enjoy pouring over the pictures, but getting all these flyers means he'll have to snatch fewer piles of *Seven Days* outside the Moosehead Diner to start his woodstove.

Jeeter is no stranger to technology: an abandoned VHF antenna is draped with his long johns and tee shirts drying in the sun. A neighbor's discarded ten-foot satellite dish lies buried in his lawn, where it hosts a variety of local reptiles, giving Jeeter thirty feet of private shoreline.

One day, Ross, the reporter from the *Hardwick Gazette*, asked Jeeter if he was related to the new president. Jeeter was flattered, answering, "Not so's I know."

"Local tales suggest you might be," suggested Ross. "'S'why I got you the spit-kit—so's we'd know."

"Think?" responded Jeeter.

"You go by the name 'von Trump,' though," added Ross.

"Well, when Heb got 'em tickets to *The Sound of Music* at the Hyde Park Opera House, and he 'n' I went, and I saw how happy 'n' all 'em von Trapps was singin' 'n' all, I decided to add the 'von' to 'Trump' . . . 'sides, sounds more dignifoied."

"Good idea," agreed Ross.

❧

The following month, Jeeter went to see Ross to help him understand the official-looking letter he got from *23andMe*.

"Holy shit!" Ross bellowed. "You're the president's nephew, a 'by-blow' as they say back home. I heard one of his brother's dalliances moved to Vermont in the *Whole Earth Catalog* migration. You said your mother's name was Euphoria Trump?"

"Only knew her as Manna. She smoked a lot."

"This says you're our president's nephew. . . . What a story!"

"'S'at mean I can buy a trailer to put on my cellar hole?"

❧

After the story broke in the *Gazette* and went out on news wires, Fox, and other social media, White House spokesman Sean Spicer denounced the story to the assembled press as "more fake news from Vermont liberals. What would you expect from a state that sends a socialist to Congress?" Spicer refused to respond to further inquiries on the subject.

❧

Jeeter painted out the "von" on his mailbox and soon began receiving visits from "men in suits."

"They's carryin' lots of 'fficial-lookin' papers 'n' such," he told the *Gazette* reporter. "I din't unnerstan' a word of it, their palaver or their writin's. They 'as nice, though, al'ays complimentin' me on my livin's. One fella bumped his head wicked on m' bulkhead door as he was comin' down the steps, got blood all over 'is nice suit."

Bewildered, Jeeter shook his head slowly. "Ross, ya gotta help me sort this out. I dunno what they's askin'," he said, handing the reporter a pile of documents.

"I'll look 'em over and get back to you," Ross promised.

The following day, Ross returned and said, "Seems there's only one good option here. I'd recommend the 'remittance-man' option. Nobody admits to anything. Nobody makes any claims. You just get a monthly check for $10,000 to keep your mouth shut about being the president's nephew and give no interviews. I say, 'take it.'"

"Too much money, a hunner'd be plenny."

"We can find ways to spend the rest, get you a double-wide to live in, maybe a fishing boat and some nice lures, a new woodstove that doesn't smoke, tune your chainsaw, a car or tractor . . . you know."

"I al'ays wanted a lawn tractor to drive inta town to get m'groceries."

"You got it." Ross concluded.

⌘

Jeeter soon became Wheelock's own Aleksandr Solzhenitsyn, protected by the postmaster, town clerk, and general storekeeper from journalists as well as Trump-obsessed ideologues of all stripes.

Missy Myers, the only attorney in Hardwick, and Ross settled with the White House counsel on a lump sum of $100,000 and $5,000 monthly. Missy serves as Jeeter's executor and disburses his monthly stipend of $500 in cash, delivered by Thelma in a plain envelope. She also forwards Jeeter's first-class mail to Missy for sorting. The Jeeter Trump Trust for Real Vermonters collects and manages the additional proceeds.

Once or twice a month, Jeeter rides his new John Deere lawn tractor to Hardwick to do his trading. There's a new double-wide sitting atop his cellar hole, but Jeeter hasn't moved in yet.

Fear and Loathing at the Kitchen Table

MARIALISA CALTA

❧

WHERE THE HELL IS HUNTER S. THOMPSON when we need him? Thompson—a.k.a. the Father of Gonzo Journalism, a.k.a. Dr. Gonzo—did not waste much ink on describing food, what with the massive amounts of mescaline, LSD, ether, amphetamines, and other controlled substances, along with stupendous quantities of booze, beer, and cigarettes that he was continuously injecting/inhaling/smoking/guzzling. But in his drug-addled, hyperbolic, and hyperactive way, Thompson often managed to cut to the chase and get at some essential truths.

If the good doctor were around today, I believe he would place the Cheeto-in-Chief squarely at the center of some kind of Caligula-style debauchery, covered in blood from butchered animals, surrounded by voracious sycophants flashing sharpened incisors, and high on ibogaine, as he wrenches haunches of meat from a blazing fire to sate unquenchable and unmentionable appetites.

Instead, we are left with media reports of Trump's predilection for fast food and what seems to be a fairly serious dependence on Diet Coke. Tame, yes, but it still ain't pretty. Big Macs, Quarter Pounders, buckets of Colonel Sanders' finest, taco bowls . . . all washed down with quarts of aspartame-enhanced liquid chemicals. Remember, this is a guy who took a few moments to wax poetic about "the most beautiful piece of chocolate cake" he was eating as he launched airstrikes against Syria.

So unhand that pint of Ben & Jerry's, and drag yourself from under the covers. The best revenge is eating well. Plus, you need your strength.

While you're girding yourself for battle and defending yourself against the onslaught of disasters likely to befall us during the current administration—unchecked effects of climate change, the evaporation of affordable health care, runaway inflation, a steep rise in food prices due to draconian restrictions on immigrant workers—you might as well cut back on consumption of current events and spend your extra time in the garden. At the very least, join a CSA or support the local farmers' market and food co-op. We're gonna need these growers. For all of his "America First"–isms, eating locally is not on Agent Orange's agenda. But it is on ours.

Bottom line? We really should "Eat More Kale"[5] . . . and anything else we can grow or buy locally or find from a reliable and sustainable source.

If you believe in the healing powers of food, now is the time to snack on foods high in feel-good tryptophan—turkey, chicken, milk, oats cheese, soy, nuts, peanut butter—or wholegrain carbs that help the brain to produce serotonin. Since the B vitamins can enhance mood, chomp on pork, chicken, leafy greens, legumes, nuts, and eggs. Protein also sparks the production of brain-enhancing chemicals, so indulge in Greek-style yogurt, meat, fish, nuts, beans, eggs, and lentils.

Cook up a mess o' wholesome, Vermont-grown food, invite your pals over, and accompany your feast with some stellar craft beer or spirits or a viniferous Vermont vintage. Or take a care package of homemade goodies to the folks on the phone banks making calls to action. We can't eat our way out of this predicament, but we can vow to weather it and to make ourselves healthier, stronger, and more fit to deal with the devastation that continues to come our way and that will surely be left behind.

5 See: https://www.eatmorekale.com/.

And if you have to get under the covers with that pint of ice cream, at least pick a brand that is truly local, and not one owned by a multinational corporation (cough, Ben & Jerry's, cough). Strafford Creamery vanilla, topped with Goat's Milk Caramel Sauce from Fat Toad Farm, might hit the spot.

To quote Dr. Gonzo: "Res ipsa loquitur. Let the good times roll."[6]

---

6 Hunter S. Thompson, Generation of Swine—*Gonzo Papers, Vol. 2: Generation of Swine: Tales of Shame and Degradation in the '80s* (Summit Books, 1988).

"Competence among the Rocks"[7]: Vermont Toolbox

BILL MARES

❧

Vermonters are not defenseless against Trump. We have a long history of inventiveness and gadgetry. The New England saying still applies to Vermonters: "Use it up, wear it out, make it do, or do without."

These tools will help us get through the next four years.

- *A lie detector*—There's only one setting, "LIES," and the needle points to it constantly and/or goes off as soon as he begins to speak.

- *Needle-nosed pliers*—For extracting tiny lies. Rarely used.

- *Backyard manure spreader*—For what flows like lava from the White House. This machine runs perpetually on the methane from the manure.

- *"Duck and cover" manual*—To "duck and cover" was the government's suggestion for how individuals should respond to a surprise nuclear attack. An official 1951 U.S. civil defense film, *Duck and Cover*, was intended primarily for children; the proper way to duck and cover is demonstrated by Bert the Turtle.

---

7 Comment upon New England farmers by Timothy Dwight, president of Yale College in *Travels in New England and New York*, vol. 1 (London: William Baynes & Son, 1823).

- *Audience "raspberry" meter*—For measuring the outrage about Trump's "lie of the day."

- *Hearing aids (minus the batteries)*—For giving Trump fans the impression that you're listening.[8]

- *Moral compass*—Take it near the White House and watch it whirl right out of its case.

- *Vermont Army Knife (not to be confused with a Swiss Army Knife)*—The Vermont version of this iconic tool is considerably more practical. It consists of both large and small razor-sharp blades that can be used to shred Trump's numerous lies. The corkscrew is invaluable for twisting and turning his words in hopes of finding a semblance of truth (not that it'll ever happen). The solid gold toothpick is a must for eliminating tiny bits and pieces of Trump's bad food served at Mar-a-Lago. The special tweezers can be used to extract the miniscule piece of truth from the truckload of lies.

- *"Long-timer's stick"*—As in Vietnam, where U.S. soldiers made notches to keep track of their days in-country until they flew home safely. This one, made of Vermont ash or maple, will carry you through 2020.

- Copy of the Vermont Constitution—The fundamental body of laws which has served Vermont well, first as an independent nation from 1777 to 1791 and, with a few changes, as a state since then.

---

8 Hearing aids also come with a sleep mask.

The Drink of the People

Bill Mares

I am a firm believer in the people. If given the truth, they can be depended upon to meet any national crisis. The great point is to bring them the real facts, and beer.

— A. Lincoln

❧

THERE ARE PLENTY OF GOOD WINES, ciders, and distilled spirits in Vermont, but good beer is one of best antidotes for political disappointment and dismay. Over one hundred years ago, the English poet A. E. Houseman penned some lines that could apply to the current occupant of the White House:

Oh many a peer of England brews
Livelier liquor than the Muse,
And malt does more than Milton can
To justify God's ways to man.
Ale, man, ale's the stuff to drink
For fellows whom it hurts to think.

I have been a home brewer for forty-five years. I sponsored the law that legalized brew pubs in Vermont. Jeff illustrated all three editions of my book about the then nascent, now mature, craft beer industry, which has grown to almost 5,000 breweries in the United States. Vermont has become one of America's beer Meccas. We go back and forth with Oregon—another blue state, we might add—for being Number 1 in the number of breweries per capita. Indeed, there are several breweries which make their beer entirely from Vermont ingredients. As one brewer says, this is the way we help other businesses succeed, and through that, the community at large.

To be sure, there are over fifty excellent breweries in Vermont, but these stand out:

The Alchemist
Foam Brewers
Hill Farmstead Brewery
House of Fermentology[9]
Lawson's Finest

---

9 Why HoF? I'm an owner, that's why!

These Hallowed Grounds

BILL MARES

❧

Unlike the insecure Trump, we don't need to make Vermont great "again"—it was never UNgreat! These places and institutions are just a few stitches in the community fabric that make Vermont, Vermont. (There are scores more.)

Seyon Pond—Groton
Vermont Symphony Orchestra—Everywhere
Thunder Road—Barre
Tunbridge World's Fair—Tunbridge
Miss Lyndonville Diner—Lyndonville
Socialist Labor Party Hall—Barre
Ground Hog Opry—Morrisville
Fourth of July Parade—Warren
Town Libraries—Everywhere
Center for Cartoon Studies—White River Junction
Fairbanks Museum—St. Johnsbury
Our motto: Freedom and Unity
Smugglers' Notch—Cambridge
Plainfield Bookstore—Plainfield
Clemmons Family Farm—Charlotte

Dairy Cows—Everywhere
Dog Mountain—St. Johnsbury
Sense of Humor—Everywhere
Vermont Arts Council—Everywhere
Vermont Humanities Council—Everywhere
Strolling of the Heifers—Brattleboro
Mad River Glen—Fayston
The State House—Montpelier
Lakefront—Burlington
Gilfeather Turnip Festival—Wardsboro
Bread and Puppet Theater—Glover
Snake Mountain—Addison and Weybridge
Vermont Vaudeville Show—Hardwick
Ice-Out at Joe's Pond—West Danville
Brattleboro Food Co-op—Brattleboro
Mad River Glen—Fayston
The Battenkill River—Arlington
St. Johnsbury Atheneum—St. Johnsbury
Vermont Cheese, Wine, Spirits, and Coffee[10]—Everywhere
Ben and Jerry's Ice Cream—Waterbury
Vermont Pub and Brewery—Burlington
Camel's Hump—Chittenden County
Bread Loaf Writers Conference—Ripton
Old Stone House—Brownington
Rokeby Museum—North Ferrisburgh

---

10 For Vermont beer, see p. 44

Why I Marched for Science

Dr. Harry Chen, MD

❧

IN 1970 we celebrated the first Earth Day. I remember it vividly, having been a college student at the University of Michigan. The energy of the first Earth Day, focused on the alarming rate of deterioration of our environment, helped lead to landmark changes in policy such as creation of the Environmental Protection Agency, and the Clean Air, Clean Water, and Endangered Species Acts.

Earth Day is now a worldwide event observed in almost 200 countries. This is a clear statement that we are all in it together and that a healthy environment is a common good. Today this shared commitment is at risk; we must reaffirm the important underpinnings of those vital roles of government.

As a physician, former Vermont commissioner of health, and soon-to-be Peace Corps volunteer in Sub-Saharan Africa, I have relied and will continue to rely on science as my guide for medical and policy decisions. In the age of Google, fake news, and deep distrust of government institutions, it's easy to lose track of the truth that science brings to us. This is the case whether the topic be vaccinations, climate change, or the latest "Ebola" that comes knocking on our door.

Health and medicine, like the environment, depend on science to drive good policy. Given this, what is my charge to those of us who are scientists?

First, become an activist—something that we may not be comfortable with or that we may not have been trained to do, but something that is vital in our country at this point. Spell out in plain language what the science says, even when it may not be popular. Be transparent with any potential conflicts we may have, and shine a light on potential conflicts and sources of support behind those on the other side of issues—pharmaceutical or energy or tobacco companies, for example. It is important that we clearly acknowledge but do not overemphasize areas of uncertainty.

Second, be empathetic with dissenters but firm in our conclusions on issues: climate change is real, vaccinations work, smoking causes cancer and heart disease, addiction is a brain disease, and sugar-sweetened beverages cause obesity. Denial stems from an individual's strongly-held beliefs and values—we must understand this as we work to make headway on important public health priorities.

Finally, do it over and over again. Repetition is an evidence-based strategy—and we have to do it together, as the whole of the science community is undoubtedly greater than the sum of its parts. I saw the strength in numbers during the most recent immunization debate in 2015. Don't get discouraged and lose the battle of wills. And remember that passion is important—but it's not personal.

Science must speak truth to power and money in a factual, nonpartisan way. In this era of Citizens United, speaking the truth in a way that gets heard is a steep hill to climb, and it requires an "all hands on deck" effort on our part. Truthfully, there is a lot of power in money.

Climate change is a human health priority and one of the key areas now under attack. Climate change is a certainty. How do we know this? Science and scientists.

In Vermont, as elsewhere, we have hotter summers, harsher winters, earlier springs, and more precipitation. Just to cite one of many alarming changes: the temperature of Lake Champlain has increased between five and seven degrees in the past fifty years. Extreme weather events occur more often. In May of 2011, I had been health commissioner for only a few months when heavy spring rains caused rising rivers, evacuations, and extensive road damage in northern and central Vermont. Lake Champlain's waters rose, flooding playgrounds, homes, and

Burlington's downtown waterfront for weeks. But this was small potatoes compared to what occurred on August 28. Tropical Storm Irene flooded a large part of the state—we lost six lives, homes were destroyed, drinking water was contaminated, and at least 500 miles of roads and 200 bridges were damaged and impassable. Access to medications, as well as hospital and health care, was limited for a time. We bear the physical and emotional scars of Irene to this day. The May storm and Tropical Storm Irene were only two of the eighteen federally-declared disasters in Vermont over the past decade.

Climate change means more illness and more deaths in Vermont. We've seen a dramatic rise in the number of blue-green algae blooms, drinking water contamination, the incidence of asthma, and the prevalence of ticks and Lyme disease. When I first came to Vermont in 1988, virtually all Lyme disease came by car from Connecticut. Today we have some of the highest case rates of Lyme infection in our nation.

Climate change does not affect people equally. Everyone is at risk, but people who spend a lot of time outdoors, those with health sensitivities, and people with limited financial and social resources are more affected. Where do the greatest carbon dioxide emissions on earth come from? China and the United States. Where will the greatest impacts on human health occur? Sub-Saharan Africa. There, the health effects (famine, disease, drought, and extreme heat) literally threaten human existence.

Here in the United States, how many more Flint, Michigans, or North Bennington, Vermonts, will we see before we reaffirm a clear commitment to clean water for all our citizens? In Flint, it took a fearless pediatrician and scientists from Virginia Tech to expose the lead in the water that was endangering Flint's most vulnerable citizens. I met Dr. Mona Attisha-Hutt, and she is a true hero. We all need to be like Dr. Attisha-Hutt, using science and raising our voices to confront power in order to protect our citizens' health and well-being.

There is hope—and we all can take actions to reduce the risks. Start by supporting science, listening to science, acting according to science. Pay attention to the challenges to science, and when you see them, clearly articulate the science as we know it, early and often.

When your defense of science seems to fall on deaf ears, say it again, louder. Say it as if your life depends on it—indeed it might.

Donald Trump, the Ultimate Invasive Species

BILL MARES

✿

ARE YOU FEELING SICK? Join the club. A society that would elect Donald Trump President is a sick society. Those who didn't vote to elect Donald Trump are waking up each day with flu-like symptoms. Nausea is the Number-One feeling for most Americans. Even before Inauguration Day, he was proclaiming his *own* Hippocratic Oath of "First, do harm!" Followed closely by "Deny that I said what I just said."

Many Vermonters are sickened by his outrages. Some have contracted TIAD—Trump-Induced Anxiety Disorder.[11] They have been vexed with virulent teeth-gnashing, not only causing them many sleepless nights but also mornings of awakening to disturbing piles of tiny pieces of enamel on their pillow. They have caught DDS, Donald Denial Syndrome—caused by a virus that causes one to go blind after looking at him too much.

But wait a minute. We are not the only ones who need medical help. Think of all the maladies afflicting Mr. Big himself. Take some pleasure in how Trump, the Common Scold, has turned the White House into his own Center for Disease Control. There are far too many diseases to be listed in their entirety. Therefore, we'll only name a few:

---

11 We're indebted to film director Sam Friedlander for this one as well as the recommended cure: *Impeachara.*®

- *Weaselitis*—a Trump-inflicted illness causing one to habitually blame everyone but oneself for one's own behavior.

- *Malignant narcissism*—when a chronic, incurable narcissist devolves to the degree that he actually likes Kim Jong Un's hairstyle.

- *Electiontosus*—common symptoms include the inability to cease talking about having won an election, resulting in the patient being unable to carry on a conversation on any other subject (with the possible exception of hairstyles).

- *Chicken Fox*—an incurable addiction to watching Fox News and feeling compelled to "tweet" about each and every piece of misinformation.

- *Trumpago*—lower-back pain caused by too much time in a golf cart.

- *Perceptosis*—incurable predilection for perception over reality.

- *Chronic infantigo*—a rare disease of stunted growth; typically, the patient projects the maturity of a three-year-old. Symptoms include, but are not limited to, tantrums when you don't get your way and chronic "tweeting" about how horrible people are constantly hurting your feelings.

- *Turrets syndrome*—an obscene obsession with the military and all things "tough-guy."

- *Ijustdontlikeitosis*—virulent scorn for public institutions, like the courts, which one cannot control and/or abolish.

- *Parasitic alternative reality*—afflicts his entire administration.

- *Incurable lack of curiosity*—he's proud that he reads no books.

Vermont Knows What Donald Trump Doesn't: Health Care Is Complicated

Dr. Joseph Hagan, MD

❧

"IN A SHORT PERIOD OF TIME I understood everything there was to know about health care," Donald Trump told *Time* magazine. Really? His mantra of "Repeal and replace" confirms that he is a know-nothing in regard to the nation's health care, and he certainly does not understand Vermont's path-breaking work in the field.

In 1989 Vermont introduced its Dr. Dynasaur Medicaid expansion for children. Prior to Dr. Dynasaur, 56,000 Vermont kids under age eighteen were uninsured and could not access medical or dental care. Dr. Dynasaur was the first Medicaid expansion in the country to utilize matching federal Medicaid dollars to cover children from birth to age eighteen if they resided in a household making under 300 percent of the federally defined poverty level.

Dynasaur was a huge success. Today, fewer than 1,000 young Vermonters lack health insurance. Other states have followed our lead. But every Trumpcare proposal so far *caps* federal Medicaid dollars to states in a "block grant." Block granting actually limits matching dollars and thwarts expansion of coverage for families in need. Can't he understand *that*?

In our state, we care about health care for all of our kids, yet we also understand that an affordable, high-quality health care system that works means caring for all of our adults, too.

Even thirty years ago, when the phenomenal cost of drugs put a drag on our state's health care budget, we had an answer! In 1989, then–U.S. Representative Bernie Sanders was already a vocal opponent of "Big Pharma." He fought for those who did not have prescription drug insurance, which at the time included every Vermonter age sixty-five and older who was insured by Medicare. In true Vermont fashion—remember, Smugglers' Notch was named for activities preceding the War of 1812—Sanders took busloads of Vermonters across the international border to purchase high-quality drugs at much lower cost in Canada. It was a *Vermont* solution for a fortunate few, but a problem still vexing the entire nation.

In the early 1990s Vermont sought to further expand coverage to include uninsured adults. A health care system that relies on hospital emergency departments for the care of the uninsured is expensive care indeed, and our little state determined that when most, if not all, Vermonters had access to health care by having access to health insurance, then costs could be contained. Preventive care would keep our population healthy, and many illnesses could be addressed in early, less complicated stages. And importantly, the state then enjoyed a substantial budget surplus. There was enough money for us to move forward on a statewide health plan.

Then in January of 1993 Bill Clinton took office having championed health care reform in his campaign. In announcing the Health Security Act that same month, he promised his health care plan would provide every American with "health care that's always there." Vermont's leaders logically paused to see what the federal government solution would be.

Sadly, there was *no* federal solution. In a preview of Trump's scorched-earth approach, significant business interests fought the employer mandate for coverage and, with the help of the health-insurance industry and Big Pharma, crushed the plan they dubbed "Hillarycare." And in Vermont, as a recession devoured surplus dollars, even our committed legislative will could not overcome the constraints of cost.

Yet Vermont's commitment to care for each of its people, to provide the highest-quality health care, and to contain costs has continued. Charged with this triple goal, the newly formed Green Mountain Care Board took the innovative approach of fostering systems of care in its regulatory oversight. State support of medical homes showed immediate success in the care of chronic health conditions. Senator Sanders champions "Medicare for all," and here in Vermont a single-payer system remains a very real possibility. We embraced the Affordable Care Act (ACA), also known as Obamacare, and have implemented ACA-mandated Accountable Care Organizations (ACOs) to strengthen our state system.

On February 27, 2017, President Trump told fellow Republicans on Capitol Hill, "Nobody knew health care could be so complicated!" Way back when he was working for his dad and was married to Ivana, Vermonters could have told him that it's complex—*hugely* complex! Now, President Trump—what part of this state's long history of action on health care do you *not* understand?

Trump on the Farm

JEFF DANZIGER

❧

WARMING UP THE HOUSE

SPREADING MANURE

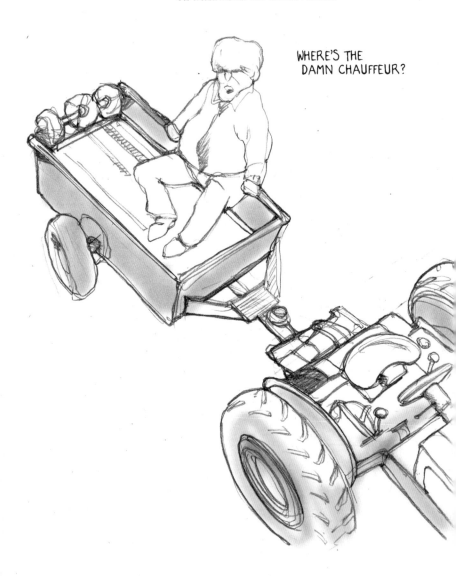

SHOVELING SNOW

GARDENING

GROW!

RUNNING A CHAIN SAW

"Green Mountain Greenies" Abhor "Drain the Swamp" Trumpbeat

DON HOOPER

❧

ESCHEWING OBFUSCATION, Trump's sycophantic follow-ers urge their brazen boss at every rally to "DRAIN THE SWAMP! DRAIN THE SWAMP!" Approaching "Lock Her Up" decibels, Trump's base makes clear with its full-throated incantations that they are on board with his pave-everything predilections. Doncha think a Trump Tower atop Camel's Hump might elevate both Vermont's humble Hump and our self-aggrandizing Bully-in-Chief to Ozymandias-scale irony?

Understandably, tree-hugging, eco-minded Vermonters—even the camo-clad crowd—don't embrace the "Drain the Swamp" program. Victory Bog? Dead Creek? Green River Reservoir? Marshfield? Vernal pools? The legislative quagmire? How 'bout Fenway Park? All are swamps by another name, right? Drain 'em? Not even the most truculent, recalcitrant Vermonter, or dyspeptic Yankee fan, would pull the plug on every iconic glade, slough, and morass in this soggy state.

From the get-go, therefore, Vermonters have been Trump-wary. We're a gentler, live-and-let-live kinda tribe. We stop for salamanders on rainy spring roadways. We fish for brookies, but

WALKING ON WATER WASN'T BUILT IN A DAY

we never exceed legal limits. Instead of asphalting every class-4 road, practical Green Mountaineers use two-wheel drive to get stuck, then four-wheel drive to get unstuck from the muddy mires that seize our rocker panels. Drain the Swamp? (And then, presumably, Pave It?) Not so much.

In anthologies, Vermont's revered Robert Frost beckons us: "I'm going out to clean the pasture spring; / I'll only stop to rake the leaves away / (And stop to watch the water clear, I may): / I sha'n't be gone long.—You come too." Now that's a Vermont mantra about water, respect, and neighborliness, all in a stanza that drowns out even the shrill cry of "DRAIN THE SWAMP."

But back to science-challenged Trump and his climate-denial psychosis. Remember that dog-eared shibboleth hanging above the office copy machine? "When you're up to your ass in alligators, it's tough to remember your original goal was to drain the swamp." Well, thanks to the Russian kleptocracy of Vladimir Putin, the Sergey twins (Kislyak and Lavrov), and their vassals Michael Flynn, Paul Manafort, Carter Page . . . and who knows whom else, Donald J. Trump is truly up to his ample ass in alligators. Now, Vermonters, who coddle endangered species (rattlesnakes, not black flies), will consider it a sign of good character to welcome alligators when climate change infuses our rivers with them. We'll prosper, too, by selling beach-front property when the Atlantic Ocean rises and laps at our camps in Rochester, Warren, and Londonderry.

Proud of our variegation, Vermont greenies will undoubtedly appropriate three homegrown hues to survive Trump:

1. *Passive-Aggressive:* As our beloved "Green Monster" Champy (now you see 'im, now you don't) would urge, "When they come 'round takin names, just freakin' disappear." Like billboards. That worked.

2. *Question Authority:* The Green Mountain Boys would say "Fight like crazy. Resist, you blockheads. Use all your weapons. Clobber the dunderhead with Act 250. Under Criterion Somethinorother, Trump probably couldn't even get a visa to visit Vermont."

3. *Syrup Drench:* Don't waterboard him; drench him in maple syrup. Sweet's the key. And drench, don't drown. Kermit the Frog, who's about as green as they get, would say: "Doesn't our five-cent bottle-deposit law of forty-some years pretty much prove that everyone makes money off environmental commonsense?"

Years ago, was Edward Abbey talking to us Vermonters about surviving Trump when he admonished us to "ramble out yonder . . . bag the peaks . . . run the rivers . . . contemplate the precious stillness?" I think so. Abbey promised us sweet victory over "those desk-bound men and women with their hearts in a safe-deposit box, and their eyes hypnotized by desk calculators." He promised that we "will outlive the bastards."

Pumping Lead
in the White House Gym

BILL MARES

❧

WE NEED TO STAY IN SHAPE during the Trump era. It's refreshing to find that on exercise, Trump has led the way. Let's visit the White House basement, not to see the bowling alley that Richard Nixon loved so much, but the gym, where President Trump has installed the latest equipment and devised his own particular sets of exercises for when he is not playing golf. He begins with Deep Seething. Then he moves on to his other routines. Here's a partial list:

- Lip curls, into sneers, snarls and scowls
- The Putin chest press (shirtless, if possible)
- Running backwards
- Lying in every position
- Dumbbells Sessions
- Clean the jerk
- Pelvic grab 'n' go
- Another cleansing round of deep seething
- Executive order roll-backs
- "Scaramucci Side-step . . . used on all issues!"

My Way (The Trumpified, Sorry Frank, UnVermont Version)

AL BORIGHT

❧

The fake press is the one that fills the air with rants and hootin',
They've taken all the fun out of my bromance with Putin.
I've lived my life for me, a highwayman without a highway,
If a Vermont sap is flowing free, just send him my way.

Regrets, I've got a bunch, I should have cronies unlike Bannon,
Dont forget 'twas my first hunch to fire Comey from a cannon.
It's loyalty that works for me, it's only "my way or the highway,"
And if you see a chick-a-dee, just send her my way.

Yes, there were times, the Woodchucks all knew
That I bit off more than I could chew,
To prove my ignorance complete,
One only needs to watch me tweet,
To the lawful word I give the bird and do it my way.

I've run a con all of my life, a life of bombast and bluster,
I've got big plans for my Kingdom[12] fans though I lead like
    General Custer.
I'll denigrate all those I hate and I must say, not in a shy way
Truth is, I burned my tax returns, and did it my way.

What is a man, why is he free, if not to slave for those like me,
No need to put on airs, I'm here to serve us billionaires.
Line up the ducks, make sure the bucks keep coming my way.

---

12 Vermont's Northeast Kingdom, that is.

A Vermont Pet
For The White House:
A Proposal

ED KOREN

❧

"Of all the stains besmirching the Trump presidency . . .
none looms so large as the absence of a White House pet."

New York Times, April 16, 2017

No TWO- OR FOUR-LEGGED ANIMAL COMPANION would be more suitable for Mr. Trump than the Vermont Turkey. This problematic fowl would be both physically and temperamentally a true and faithful sidekick to his master. Starting with the turkey's physical presence—its wattle (the flap of skin under its chin), its caruncles (fleshy bumps that grow on its head and throat), and its snood (the fleshy flap hanging from its beak) this bird would more than complement his master's corporeal presence and lurching gait and demeanor. The colors of the head and neck—red, blue and white—could give a well needed boost to his master's unconvincing patriotism (while expressing loyalty by mirroring the signature red tie.)

Further reason to believe this to be a brilliant pairing is the behavior of the Turkey: its polygamous relationships and male displays that would tickle his owner's fancy, as well as its tendency of puffing feathers, spreading tail, and dragging wings.

And clinching the case for this inspired mutual companionship is that the American people could consider both pet and master in the same light—as naïve, stupid, and inept—although the Vermont Turkey has a great many redeeming features as well.

"Trump Is Champ. Champ Is Trump."

SALLY POLLAK

❧

THE LAKE CHAMPLAIN MONSTER-cum-president is on the prowl in Vermont. The creature that was spotted by a sea captain two centuries ago "with a red tie around its neck" has emerged from the depths of the lake onto *terra firma*, Vermont style.

The tie remains conspicuous, swinging to and fro as Trump makes the rounds in the Green Mountain State. Catch him if you can. Sightings include:

Stowe Mountain Resort

The lift lines are super-long—never longer!—the day Trump straps on a snowboard to shred his way down the side of Mount Mansfield, Vermont's highest peak.

The seventy-one year-old president has difficulty mastering the alpine sport—"I don't stand by anything!" he announces—an apparent reference to the fact that he keeps falling down. *Splat!* on his rear end.

Speculation arises that his bone spurs are back and causing balance trouble, a return of the pesky medical problem that kept him out of the army a half century ago. It's possible, however, that Trump simply prefers to be bottom-down on his Burton board. For his outing at Stowe, the president has mounted a vintage piece from Burton's 2008 Love series: a snowboard decorated with a mostly naked Playboy bunny.

"I stand by this!" Trump enthuses, showing off his gear.

Ekwanok Country Club in Manchester

On a golden summer day in a Vermont "gold" town,[13] Trump is playing golf at Ekwanok Country Club. His golf partner is a tall man with chiseled-granite features—a local—who has come to the course from a nearby country estate called Hildene.[14]

He wants to challenge the Champ.

As the round starts, the two men make small talk—the weather, the dress code, the club's exalted place in the golf world—before turning serious about matters of state.

"What's up with the Civil War?" Trump asks the big fellow. "Couldn't you find a way around that one?"

His partner says nothing.

On the back nine, breaking inquisitive ground with a question most people don't ask, Trump persists: "Why *was* the Civil War? There were a few bad hombres, that's a surety. But gimme a break. Why the war? You could have settled their differences!"

The tall man keeps his eyes on the ball and the distant greens.

Desperate, Trump shouts at him, while other golfers gape.

The tall man looks down at his opponent and says, "You got the wrong guy. I'm not Andrew Jackson!"

Dacha in Cavendish

Behind the barbed-wire fence of a wooded compound in Cavendish, Trump is learning to live the country life. Internet access is slow and spotty, media attention nonexistent—and Trump is itching for action.

He wants to make contact with the former occupant of the home—a reclusive writer from Russia. When he's greeted with silence from Solzhenitsyn (who died in 2008), Trump grows increasingly frustrated and dismayed.

---

13 I.e., a wealthy town taxed higher to help pay for a poorer town's schools.
14 Estate founded by Robert Todd Lincoln, only surviving son of President Abraham Lincoln.

He decides to forego efforts at oral communication and reach the novelist through the written word. Trump leaves his dacha for the Cavendish Town Hall, where he tweets out a message:

"@Alexander," he types.

Oops!

"@Aleksandr," Trump tries again. "Gulag sounds rough! Let's talk rubble to rubles. Jared will set up a terrific hideaway! Ready to deal in VT!"

Lakeside Sanctuary

Things got too hot, literally, for Trump in Vermont. Brushing up on his French—"*Triste! Merde!*"—he beats a path north toward the wall-less border.

But he grows weary on his way, and seeks refuge at a sanctuary on the shores of Lake Champlain—a 350-year-old place of worship called St. Anne's Shrine.

Spiritual seekers in silent retreat are astonished by the arrival of the hot, the tired, the grumpy Trump. Recognizing an hombre in distress, they grill a steak, squeeze ketchup on it, and offer the traveler a room where he can rest. He is sent to bed with two scoops of ice cream.

The still of the night is disrupted by a splash and the crash of waves. In the morning, scanning the horizon, parishioners are certain they see a monster in the lake.

Map of Vermont

LARRY FEIGN

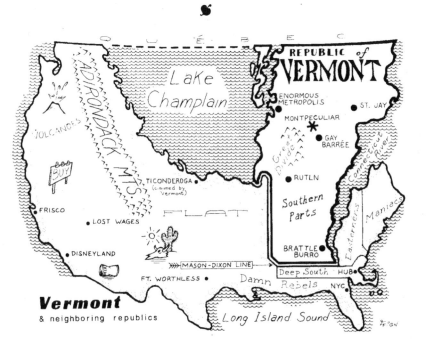

The Vermont Economy

Eric Hanson

❧

L ET'S TALK FOR A MINUTE about the Vermont Economy. You can be sure that we are going to be affected big time by the fiscal proposals of President Trump. This might mean an economic bonanza—ah, hope springs eternal—but more likely it's going to feel like a solid uppercut to the jaw. Ugh. So we had better get ready.

Vermont is a quirky place. It has always been tough here— eight months of winter and four months of rough sledding. But our people are independent-minded, our roads are not clogged, our skies are azure blue, and our small size means we can govern in a civil and measured way.

We have a lot of talent here in the state, including in economics. David Hale may be the most brilliant economic mind Vermont has produced. He was born in St. Johnsbury in 1951, educated at St. J Academy, Georgetown University, and the London School of Economics. He became a bona fide, certified economic expert who has advised governments and investors worldwide.

Back in high school, he began writing economic opinion pieces for the *Stowe Reporter*. But he also poked fun at himself and the state, joking that his family had been going downhill for seven generations as they moved from the high-hill farmsteads of the Northeast Kingdom to lower ones and finally to running a retail store in downtown St. Johnsbury.

Unfortunately, David died in 2015, so we shall never know how his predictions and advice for Vermont would play out today.

Historically, Vermont has been pretty close to the end of the economic pipeline. We did, of course, have our heydays—sheep farming in the 1800s, hydro-powered manufacturing including woolen mills and machine tools, and yes, plenty of cows, plenty of milk, and plenty of small farms. But life is not always easy for Vermont's inhabitants. When John Steinbeck wrote *Travels with Charley: In Search of America* back in 1960, the Vermont he drove through still had very distinct regions, distinct accents, and distinct economics. But no longer—Vermont has become homogenized like much of the rest of the country.

With the coming of the interstate highways in the 1960s and the changes in communications, the Vermont economy became much more homogenous and much more similar to the rest of the United States. Immigration brought many "flatlanders from

away." Today, if you break down the percentages of Vermonters employed in agriculture, manufacturing, services, etc., the state looks pretty much like the rest of the country. Some differences but not many.

However, Vermont battles its own unique economic headwinds. We are a small state whose largest city, Burlington, has only 40,000 residents. Younger people and newer companies often like to congregate in bigger cities with more employment opportunities. If you come to Vermont for a niche job, you risk having to leave the state if that job doesn't work out. We have the jobs, just not very many in each specialty.

Vermont also has some self-inflicted challenges. Like high taxes. Some see this as a badge of honor that reflects on our high level of services and quality of life. Others disagree, saying we have champagne taste on a beer income. In addition to high taxes, there are tough environmental regulations to protect the state's physical beauty that add time and costs to economic growth. Natural beauty does indeed have its price, one that Vermonters have been willing to shoulder.

But our biggest economic challenge is demographic. People-wise, we just aren't growing. We have a low birth rate and, on balance, out-migration. We could compensate by attracting more New Americans—but the Trump Administration is definitely not on the same page on this issue.

So what can we do? In the words, and in some cases the spirit, of David Hale, and with a definite twinkle in our eye, here are some real Vermont ideas for strengthening the state's economy.

David liked the idea of returning to our roots. So how about establishing a state flock of sheep? Remember the book *Real Vermonters Don't Milk Goats*? Well, often things that go around actually do come around. Vermonters are milking goats today, and we need to milk more. Sheep and goats could provide healthy summer jobs for young shepherds and shepherdesses supplied with staffs, sheepdogs, tents, and supplies. The animals could "mow" highway rights-of-way at a fraction of the cost of tractors. And just think of the marriage of nineteenth-century agriculture and twenty-first-century technology, with sheep sharing the landscape with rows of solar panels.

Another great idea is our own Fort Knox, using the worked-out granite or marble quarries as reservoirs for our liquid gold, maple syrup. And speaking of granite, how about granite chips, which range in weight from one ounce to five tons? Good for paperweights, necklaces, doorstops, and volume fillers in fish tanks and toilets, and surely these granite chips would be better than grain bags or cement blocks for putting some extra weight in your pickup.

Goddard College could be an interesting money maker. To insure fiscal stability in higher education, how about using the college as a permanent theme park of the 1960s? What tourist would not want to see hippies in original tie-dye T-shirts and beards marching in a daily protest demonstration? With Vermont on the cusp of legalizing marijuana, the nostalgia of watching an authentic re-creation of a drug bust would be irresistible.

And finally, we can provide an economic solution for Vermont's dilapidated railroads. We could marry our desperate infrastructure needs with the needs of the Defense Department, which is always trying to keep our enemies off guard. For a small fee, we could put missiles on abandoned Vermont railcars. As David might put it: if Vermont didn't know where its rail cars were, then certainly the Russians (or the North Koreans) wouldn't, either!

So take that, President Trump! If you are not going to be of any help to Vermont, we will just take things into our own hands.

Facts / Alternative
Facts — Quiz

BILL MARES

✿

1. The Bayley-Hazen Road was built during what era?
A. 1920–1940
B. 1960–1980
C. 1840–1860
D. 1760–1780

2. Who said it?
A. George Dewey
B. Stephen Douglas
C. Ira Allen
D. Dick Snelling
E. Tom Salmon
F. George Aiken
G. Otto Von Bismarck
H. Sinclair Lewis

_____ *"The best way to kill something in Vermont is to mandate it."*

_____ *"My idea of a republic is a little state in the north of your great country . . . Vermont."*

_____ *"Vermont is not for sale!"*

_____ *"You may fire when ready, Gridley!"*

_____ "Vermont is the most glorious spot on the face of the globe for a man to be born in, provided he emigrates when he is very young."

_____ "I know of no country that abounds in a greater diversity of hill and dale."

_____ "Either impeach him or get off his back!"

3. The first female lieutenant governor in the United States was a Vermonter. *True or False?*

4. The first U.S. ski tow was in what Vermont town?
A. Woodstock
B. Killington
C. Burke
D. Stowe

5. The first U.S. patent signed by George Washington was issued to a Vermonter for . . .
A. An iron stove.
B. Potash.
C. A sap boiler.
D. An oxen yoke.

6. A Vermonter was the first person to cross the United States by bicycle. *True or False?*

7. Vermont was first state to outlaw slavery. *True or False?*

8. Vermont was the first state to permit vote by absentee. *True or False?*

9. Vermont was first state to have a "normal" school. *True or False?*

10. Which federal program began in Vermont?
A. TVA
B. FDIC
C. Head Start
D. No Child Left Behind

11.   Fit the person to the nickname:

A. "The Lone Granger"   Lefevre
B. "King Reid"   Tuttle
C. "Snowflake"   Bentley
D. "Big Al"   Lee
E. "Spread Fred"   Kennedy
F. "Mean Mildred"   Arthur
G. "Spaceman"   Moulton
H. "Peanut"   Hayden (Berlin
                                              overseer of the poor)

*12. How many Democrats were elected Governor between 1860
and 1960?* _____

13. John M. Weeks of Salisbury invented . . .

A. The first egg "grader" that separates white from brown eggs.
B. The first automated gutter cleaner for dairy farms.
C. The bunker silo.
D. A beehive that saved its bees during honey extraction.

*14. Match the inventor with the invention, or discovery, he's
known for.*

A. Thomas Davenport (Brandon, 1837)
    Globe
B. Thaddeus Fairbanks (St. Johnsbury, 1830)
    Electric motor
C. Silas Hawes (Shaftsbury, 1814)
    Platform scale
D. James Wilson (Bradford, 1799)
    Steel carpenter's square

15. Put these Vermont governors in chronological order:

A. ____ Phil Hoff
B. ____ Madeleine Kunin
C. ____ Robert Stafford
D. ____ F. Ray Keyser Jr.
E. ____ Deane Davis
F. ____ George Aiken

"Little Minds Run
in the Same Ditch"

❧

*Wolfgang Mieder, professor of German and folklore at the
University of Vermont, has made a study of proverbs from around
the world and has compiled and published many collections.[15] He
has a particular love of Vermont proverbs, and so we have dug into
that special collection for appropriate comments about living with
Donald Trump. Mieder writes: "There is a certain amount of danger connected with deducing national or regional characteristics
from proverbs . . . However, proverbs do reflect to a certain degree
the worldview of their users, and with caution one could perhaps
say that [this collection] of folk wisdom current in Vermont reflects
the stereotypic view of Vermonters . . . Above all, the proverbs reflect
in concise and picturesque language a way of life which appeals to
real Vermonters and so-called flatlanders alike . . ."*

He can't speak well who always talks.

A person's speech reveals the soul.

Nobody ever repented holding his tongue.

---

15 Wolfgang Mieder, *Talk Less and Say More* (Shelburne, VT: New
England Press, 1986) and *Yankee Wisdom* (Shelburne, VT: New England
Press, 1989).

A wise man knows his own ignorance; a fool thinks he knows everything.

Never cackle unless you laying.

The more riches, the less wisdom.

You can't expect anything from a pig but a grunt.

You can't make a crooked stick lie straight.

The steam that toots the whistle never turns a wheel.

Talk less and say more.

Some people are not fit to root with a pig.

You can't keep trouble from coming, but you don't have to give it a chair to sit on.

When you argue with a fool, that makes two of you.

A handsaw is a good thing, but not to shave with.

Love your neighbor, but don't pull down the hedge.

There's no use keeping a dog and barking yourself.

Any man can strut; the pompous man struts standing still.

Vermonters Speaking Truth to Power

BILL MARES

❧

Throughout Vermont's history, its citizens have called to account the autocratic and the tyrannical, the brutal and the cruel, the hypocrites and the liars. Here is a sampler of those words.

Ethan Allen: "The gods of the hills are not the gods of the valleys."

Matthew Lyon, in a June 20, 1798, letter to Spooner's Vermont Journal *in Windsor, Vermont, that helped lead to his indictment for violating the Alien and Sedition Acts:* ". . . But whenever I shall, on the part of the Executive, see every consideration of the public welfare swallowed up in a continual grasp for power, in an unbounded thirst for ridiculous pomp, foolish adulations, and selfish avarice; when I shall behold men of real merit daily turned out of office for no other cause but independency of sentiment; when I shall see men of firmness, merit, years, abilities, and experience, discarded in their applications for office, for fear they possess that independence, and men of meanness preferred, . . . I shall not be their humble advocate."

Gen. John Sedgwick, at the Battle of Gettysburg: "Put the Vermonters ahead and keep everything well closed up."[16]

Another Vermonter, the nineteenth-century lawyer Edward J. Phelps, once remarked: "You can find men that will face the batteries; you will find very few that will face majorities, few who will stand up against the pressure of an erroneous, an excited, and a deluded popular opinion; few that are not afraid to be left alone, like children in the dark. . . ."

George Perkins Marsh: "Man is everywhere a disturbing agent. Wherever he plants his foot, the harmonies of nature are turned to discords."

Lord James Bryce: "You men of northern Vermont . . . living among its rocks and mountains in a region which may be called the Switzerland of America—you are a people here who have had hearts full of love of freedom which exists in mountain people and who have the indomitable spirit and unconquerable will which we always associated with the lake and mountain lands."[17]

General Oliver O. Howard: "As to the second reason, any feeling of personal resentment towards the late Confederates I would not counsel or cherish. Our countrymen—large numbers of them—combined and fought us hard for a cause. They failed and we succeeded; so that, in an honest desire for reconcilement, I would be the more careful, even in the use of terms, to convey no hatred or reproach for the past. Such are my real convictions, and certainly the intention in all my efforts is not to anger and separate, but to pacify and unite."

Senator George Aiken, describing why it is good to have political enemies: "You have got to have enemies to get votes, but you have to be careful to pick the right ones. I picked the railroads and the utilities and they were the best enemies I ever could have had."

---

16 Cited in a speech by T. McMahon Martin, Adjutant General, Sixth Army Corps, at Vermont Officers Society, Montpelier, Vermont, November 11, 1880.
17 British Ambassador to the United States Lord James Bryce, in a speech July 8, 1909, upon the Tercentenary celebration of the discovery of Lake Champlain and Vermont, in *Report to the General Assembly of the State of Vermont* (Montpelier, VT: Capital City Press, 1910).

Senator James M. Jeffords: "I became a Republican not because I was born into the party, but because of the kind of fundamental principles that [Ernest Gibson, George Aiken, Ralph Flanders, and Bob Stafford] and many other Republicans stood for—moderation, tolerance, and fiscal responsibility. Their party—our party—was the party of Lincoln . . .

"Aiken and Gibson and Flanders and Stafford were all Republicans. But they were Vermonters first. They spoke their minds, often to the dismay of their party leaders, and did their best to guide the party in the direction of our fundamental principles. . . .

"Increasingly, I find myself in disagreement with my party. . . .

"Looking ahead, I can see more and more instances when I will disagree with the president [George W. Bush] on very fundamental issues: issues of choice, the direction of the judiciary, tax-and-spend decisions, missile defense, energy, the environment and education. . . .

"In order to best represent my state of Vermont, my own conscience, and the principles I have stood for my whole life, I will leave the Republican Party and become an Independent."[18†]

Jody Williams,[19] in an interview with Real Leaders *magazine in 2015:* "The image of peace with a dove flying over a rainbow and people holding hands singing 'Kumbaya' ends up infantilizing people who believe that sustainable peace is possible. If you think that singing and looking at a rainbow will suddenly make peace appear, then you're not capable of meaningful thought, or understanding the difficulties of the world."

18 James M. Jeffords, *My Declaration of Independence* (New York: Simon & Schuster, 2001), 114–16.
19 Born in Rutland and a graduate of the University of Vermont, Williams is a political activist who was awarded the Nobel Peace Prize in 1997 for her work toward the banning and clearing of anti-personnel mines.

Senator Bernie Sanders, quoted by the Huffington Post, *September 14, 2009:* "I don't recognize the raucous and rowdy town meetings in other parts of the country that have grabbed big headlines this month. Those shouters and screamers talk about 'freedom,' but what they are doing is trying to disrupt meetings. That's the absolute opposite of what freedom of discussion is about. They are trying to shout down speakers and shut down town meetings because they are afraid to debate the real issues and the unprecedented set of problems our country now faces."

Aleksandr Solzhenitsyn, in the address he prepared (but was unable to deliver) upon being awarded the 1970 Nobel Prize in Literature: "Anyone who has proclaimed violence his method inexorably must choose lying as his principle."

Governor Peter Shumlin and Governor-elect Phil Scott in a joint statement, November 2016: "At this time of national discord, Vermont can present a united voice urging compassion, commitment to community, and fierce dedication to equal rights and justice. The example we set for the nation can help guide us forward through this turbulent time.

"Vermont's reservoir of goodwill is deep and our national leadership well documented. Our history is of being first to stand up for equality, inclusiveness, and tolerance is well known. . . .

"Vermonters know how to weather the storms. When times are toughest, we always come together to focus on what's important—each other.

"Together, we'll defend the rights and freedoms of all; set an example for the nation to follow; and stand united in our commitment to move forward. The nation is counting on us to do our part—and we will."

Trump Supports Order
at Any Cost

HAVILAND SMITH

❧

In 1954, Senator Ralph Flanders (R-Vermont) led the move to censure Sen. Joseph McCarthy (R-Wisconsin) for his abuse of two senatorial committees investigating his conduct of personal attacks and wild accusations about domestic enemies. Said Flanders, "Were the junior senator from Wisconsin in the pay of the Communists, he could not have done a better job for them."

In the following essay, another Vermonter, Haviland Smith, a former CIA officer and head of its counter-terrorism unit, calls to account the far more powerful authoritarian and conspiratorialist, President Donald Trump.

AMERICA HAS NEW LEADERSHIP. Our new president has, probably compulsively and inadvertently, given us a crystal-clear picture of who he really is and of his likes and dislikes.

He has shared his views about the world leaders with whom the United States must deal and in the process has told us why he likes them and the kind of behavior he admires. What he has told us is that, first and foremost, he admires strongmen who seize power and exercise it in whatever way is necessary to maintain it, whether legal, morally acceptable, or not.

Unlike past American presidents, he somehow feels compelled to publicly express his admiration for a group of foreign leaders whose activities are so questionable that they would never have been praised by any of his predecessors.

The list of those presidentially praised and admired is endless. It includes primarily those who, at best, have terrible human rights records and employ what in this country would be seen as extrajudicial methods in order to maintain their power.

His favorites begin with Vladimir Putin of Russia and continue with Rodrigo Duterte of the Philippines, Abdel Fattah Said al-Sisi of Egypt, and Recep Tayyip Erdogan of Turkey. In addition, he has spoken admiringly, particularly in terms of the control they have exercised over their people, of Iraq's Saddam Hussein, Libya's Muammar Gaddafi, Syria's Bashar al-Assad, China's Xi Jinping, Thailand's Prayuth Chan-o-cha, and North Korea's Kim Jong Un.

Why would any president of the USA openly deal with, invite here for a visit, or speak positively of such a group? Could it possibly be that they represent precisely what our president would like to be, a powerful autocrat?

What sort of intellectual, moral, and ethical environments do these attitudes set for members of his administration and the rest of the country?

He has given us this privileged look at his own personal *modus operandi* and has told us by inference the way he would like to deal with our country. It might be wise for us to recognize that we have a new leader who quite possibly does not share our constitutional attachment to American ideals. This could represent a very real threat to many of the things in which we believe that are critical to the democratic future of our country.

And, who is the man? What is he really like? We have gotten a view of him through his own actions and statements that should well give us reason for concern. The president has shown himself to be a sexist and a religious bigot. He has further been described as immature, self-centered, spoiled, insecure, hypersensitive, impetuous, crass, crude, pompous, thoughtless, and autocratic. And on top of all that, he would appear to have difficulty telling objective truth from his own self-generated, self-serving fictions.

The result of all of this is that we are beginning to see on a national level a "new" interpersonal behavior modeled on the president's behaviors. We seem to be leaving behind the old, thoughtful, and civil ways in favor of this new, crass presidential model. We are moving forward with the concept that if the president can think, do, or say these things, why can't we?

If that turns out to be the model for our future interpersonal behavior, God help America, and Vermont!

Trump Letter to Vermont Congressional Delegation

Jasper Craven

❧

The White House
1600 Pennsylvania Avenue
Washington DC, 20009
May 10, 2017

To Vermont's Three Esteemed Congressmen:

It is with great pleasure that Melania and I seek your presence at my first congressional picnic as president, to be held on June 22 on the White House lawn. Please feel free to bring your lovely family members. Food and drinks will be served.

I look forward to meeting with you all during the festivities, and conversing about the common ground we can find to make America great again. While I know we don't see eye to eye on many matters, I have a great deal of respect for the state of Vermont and its constituents. Yours is a state of transcendent beauty, with rolling hills and peaceful waters. Your air is sweet, your soil rich.

But it's no Manhattan, believe me. My towers touch the sky and rip into the clouds. In Burlington, your wimpy mayor—Weiner-something—can barely get approval for a 160-foot redevelopment of the Church Street Mall. That would be

Vermont's tallest building!? 160 feet? Please. I have a boat longer than that.

As you all know, I visited Burlington during my presidential campaign. Performed at the Tin Theater. Beautiful venue, but no Carnegie Hall. Stuffy place, really. Not classy.

There were thousands lined up outside to see me in Burlington, and that was in the dark, desolate cold of winter. It was so frigid that night—minus 30 degrees. My people tell me there were 40,000 people who received tickets for my rally, more people than live in all of Caledonia County. A whole county saw me, and on a night when it was so cold I heard that people's Subarus didn't even start.

You people in Vermont love Subarus. Japanese cars? Please, give me a vehicle with stamina, energy, elegance.

But, overall, Vermont is a gorgeous place. Huge.

It's a state brimming with innovative entrepreneurs and fledgling businesses that are reinventing what can be produced in a small, rural state.

I'd particularly like to praise Ariel Quiros and Bill Stenger, two of the best titans of business in the state. Tremendous people. Quiros especially. He used his hard-earned cash to purchase a $2-million condo at Trump Tower. One of our best condos, I'm told.

Those two really have the business acumen of a New York real estate king like me. I'm sure they've both read *The Art of the Deal*, my second favorite book, after the Bible.

I presume Quiros and Stenger paid particular attention to the following—real—quote from the book:

"The final key to the way I promote is bravado. I play to people's fantasies. People may not always think big themselves, but they can still get very excited by those who do. That's why a little hyperbole never hurts. People want to believe that something is the biggest and the greatest and the most spectacular. I call it truthful hyperbole. It's an innocent form of exaggeration, and a very effective form of promotion."[20]

---

20 Donald J. Trump and Tony Schwartz, *The Art of the Deal* (New York: Ballantine Books, 1987). In a July 2016 *New Yorker* article about Schwartz, he describes his regrets about writing *The Art of the Deal*. On ABC's *Good Morning America*, he said he had "put lipstick on a pig."

In addition to Stenger and Quiros, your state has some other great businessmen and -women. But Ben & Jerry? Losers. Overrated. Phish Food is garbage, total trash.

Those ice cream people supported Bernie for president, a communist!

Bernie: you've got guts. But if you cross me in 2020, I will bring in the big guns. It will be over before it started. My people will be watching you at the picnic, so don't get any ideas. I heard that, during past presidential picnics, you have stolen large vats of coleslaw to "redistribute to the one percent." Not good. Pathetic!

As for Patrick Leahy, you are a man worthy of great respect. The most senior senator in the chamber, with more than four decades of public service. But I didn't appreciate your tough questioning of Attorney General Jeff Sessions during his confirmation hearings. You were so eagerly looking to take the spotlight. Sad!

I look forward to speaking with you, U.S. Representative Peter Welch, at the picnic. I have heard you worked with esteemed House Speaker Paul Ryan in the past on cheese legislation. Good! I enjoyed our March conversation on renegotiating drug prices. You made some good points, as did I. The pharmaceutical CEOs I've recently met with have also made some good points on health care policy. The head of Novartis is a member of Mar-a-Lago, home of the best coleslaw on the planet! (Don't get any ideas, Bernie.) The Johnson & Johnson CEO actually owns a summer home in Vermont and had a great joke about the state:
Q: What's the best thing to come out of Rutland?
A: Route 7

Rutland does have its troubles, and the opioid crisis is very bad. Am very happy that our Muslim ban was able to prevent 100 Syrian refugees from entering the city. The previous mayor—I call him Chris LOSERas—should not have so vigorously defended the resettlement. He lost because of it. Pathetic!

Anyways, I look forward to the Vermont delegation's presence at the picnic. (No backpacks, Bernie.)

Thank you again for your service to our country. You each bring an impressive energy to your political efforts in Washington. But not as much energy as me, believe me.

Sincerely,

Vermont's Religion

BILL MARES

❧

A PARTICULARLY RELIGIOUS GENTLEMAN from Barnet felt that eight Beatitudes were probably insufficient for leading a good life. He added one more: "Blessed is the man who, having nothing to say, abstains from giving wordly evidence of the fact."[21]

Here we are in the third-least religious state in the Union.[22] Yet we have four saints who, if you assembled their voting records, could walk on the liberal waters of Lake Champlain or the Winooski River. Below are some scriptures from Vermont's own St. George, St. Patrick, St. Peter, and St. Bernard.[23]

St. George:
If we were to wake up some morning and find everyone the same race, creed and color, we would find some other causes of prejudice by noon.

The best policy is to declare victory and leave.

---

21 Allen Foley, *What the Old-Timer Said* (Brattleboro, VT: Stephen Green Press, 1971), p. 23.
22 Defined by worship attendance, prayer frequency, belief in God, and the self-described importance of religion in one's life. (See: http://www.pewresearch.org/fact-tank/2016/02/29/how-religious-is-your-state/?state=alabama Pew Research Center.)
23 George Aiken, Patrick Leahy, Peter Welch, and Bernie Sanders.

St. Patrick:
Get fifteen Democrats in a room and you get twenty opinions.

The American public is sick and tired of being lied to.

St. Peter:
In Washington, "delay" is too often code for "derail."

There's a tendency in politics to attribute bad motivation much too quickly, and the sooner you attribute bad motivation to someone you disagree with, the harder it is to find some common ground to make some progress that would give people confidence that you've got it more right than wrong.

St. Bernard:
For many, the American Dream has become a nightmare.

At its worst, Washington is a place where name-calling, partisan politics too often trumps policy.

Living in the Age of Trump—
Life in a Bubble

Governor Madeleine M. Kunin

❧

I N THE AGE OF TRUMP, to live in Vermont is to live in a bubble.
We are blue and proud of it. On election night, Vermont was
the first state to declare the overwhelming defeat of Donald
Trump. We talk a lot about Trump. Whenever there is a chance
to eavesdrop on a conversation while sitting in a café or waiting
in line at the grocery store, we are likely to hear the name Trump,
followed by a deep sigh. His tweets are a kind of invasive species.
They populate our brains and torture our dreams.

As Vermonters, we live in a bubble. We are grateful that we do
not live in the South, the West, or the Midwest. We are pleased
that we reside in the sane and sensible Northeast, where we
converse and complain with people who are likely to agree us.
We can find Trump Republicans in Vermont, but they live in
small pockets and tend to be close-lipped. We can safely avoid
them. We have not yet suffered directly from the Trump agenda
because we have a decent state government with a Democratic
House and Senate, a moderate Republican governor who is
unafraid of Trump, and a vocal congressional delegation which
speaks clearly for us.

What does it mean to live in a bubble? Our enclosure
insulates us from the daily beat of Trump tweets and allows us

to maintain our sanity. It's good for our health. On the other hand, though, living in a bubble can lead to self-satisfaction, even complacency. We are better than the opposition, in every way. Each day that Donald Trump launches a new assault against the Obama legacy, we cringe. It looks like Trump has made a list of all of Obama's achievements and stuck a finger in our eye, as if that would kill them. It hurts, it's outrageous. And it's depressing. A thin fog of despair pervades our atmosphere.

What can we do? There is only one recourse: activism. Vermont has a history of rebellion. We fought for our beliefs during the Civil War, and the Vietnam War. After the Women's March on January 21, an innumerable number of opposition groups sprang up in Vermont, meeting in living rooms and Town Halls to oppose the Trump agenda. Many are still going strong, but some have already given up.

Living in a Vermont bubble is comforting—but it is also dangerous. No matter how attractive the bubble is, we cannot survive in it. We are not immune to what is happening in the rest of the world, or in our country. There is a major danger facing us: battle fatigue. Trump has launched a full-blown attack against so many of our beliefs and democratic values—all at once—that we find it hard to focus and fight back.

Let us pause for a minute and concentrate on one outrage: Trump's treatment of women. He has made it clear that he likes women for their bodies but not for their brains. Whenever he is photographed with members of his cabinet or his team of advisors, the picture looks like a 1950s lineup of the Rotary Club. The only women he appears to trust are his daughter and his wife, and occasionally his press secretary. He has far fewer women and minorities in his cabinet than were in the cabinet of any recent president: they add up to six out of twenty-four, fewer than those appointed by Obama, Clinton, or either of the Bushes. And they are not even in key positions. The exception is Kellyanne Conway, who coined the term "alternative facts" and has provided a heap of them.

Not only does Trump ogle women, he seeks to control them. His endorsement of far-right-wing restrictions on abortion *and* on contraception will have a devastating impact on women in America and around the globe. The fight against safe and legal abortion is the ultimate put-down of women because it implies that women are incapable of deciding for themselves whether and when they will have a child, regardless of the circumstances. In cases of incest, rape, or illness, male-dominated political institutions will decide for us. Most disturbing is Trump's restrictions on contraception. If Trump were sincere about economic growth, he would include birth control in the list of services provided in health care coverage in order to make it more possible for women to enter and remain in the workplace.

The list of Trump's offenses against women is long. The most destructive is Trump's language. His diatribes diminish women, immigrants, and minorities. His words can be brutal. Sadly, they have begun to infect our everyday dialogue. It is hard to teach our children civility when the president of the United States delights in being crude.

Yes, we can take comfort inside our Vermont bubble. But it is a delicate bubble, ready to burst at any time.

Donald Trump's Political Impact on Vermont

STEPHEN C. TERRY

❧

CONSIDER THE FOLLOWING Vermont political scene between now and the elections to be held on November 6, 2018:

If there is anything certain in life, the re-election of Senator Bernie Sanders and Representative Peter Welch should be on top of your list.

Republican governor Phil Scott, who has never supported Trump, can very likely count on serving a second term. History is on his side, since the last GOP governor denied a second term was F. Ray Keyser in 1962, when one-term Burlington House member Philip H. Hoff knocked him off to become the first Democratic governor in 109 years. Vermonters do not have a habit of kicking out their governors, although it came close to that in 2014, when Republican Scott Milne nearly defeated incumbent Democratic governor Peter Shumlin. That is why the state's highest elected Progressive/Democrat, Lieutenant Governor David Zuckerman, is unlikely to give up a secure seat to challenge Scott.

Vermont Democrats have a firm hold on the other state-wide offices: Treasurer Beth Pearce, Secretary of State Jim Condos, and Attorney General T. J. Donovan are likely to face little opposition. Democratic/Progressive auditor of accounts, Douglas Hoffer, is on his way to becoming a lifer. Of these officials, Donovan is the only statewide Democratic official, other than Sanders and Welch, who will keep challenging Trump on immigration, clean energy, and trade issues.

Democrats will also go into the November 2018 elections with commanding majorities in the Vermont House and Senate. Whether Democrats can retain some of these seats will have a lot to do with the mood of voters based on the condition of Vermont's economy on Election Day.

If voters across the state are still uneasy—that is, if the impact of the 2008 recession is still a drag on the economic and psychological outlook of Vermonters—there could be changes in the composition of the legislature. If this happens, it will be local and state issues, not national ones, that will drive voters.

Moderate Republicans, not the estimated 22,000 Vermont True Believers who backed Trump in the March 2016 presidential primary, have a shot at improving their membership in the House and Senate.

One prediction is probably safe. In order to be politically successful in Vermont, no candidate will hitch his/her wagon to an unpredictable, undisciplined horse named Trump. They will either oppose or shun him.

In Vermont, the only way a moderate Republican can win a statewide office is to be politically pro-choice, pro-environment, and pro-gay marriage. With those positions, a Republican can succeed in a liberal Democratic deep-blue state and win, advocating hold-the-line on state spending, a no-tax-increase plan, a pushing-economic-growth agenda, and opposition to gun control. What a Republican can't be, and expect to win in Vermont, is autocratic and overly partisan—in other words, a "mini-me" of Donald Trump.

Meanwhile, assuming Trump's presidential job approval continues to wallow in the mid-thirties, state Democrats and Progressives should then be able to improve their election chances in 2018 on the basic promise of protecting Vermont and its values.

A key to maintaining Vermont's deep blue will be to Bernie Sanders' ability to help Vermont Democrats and Progressives produce a heavy voter turnout in 2018. How much time will Sanders spend in Vermont, given his desire to campaign across the country for congressional candidates in the 2018 mid-term elections? Nothing would embarrass Sanders more than Vermont's deep-blue map turning purple. If Sanders has ambitions to run for president again in 2020, assuming that Trump is still around to run for a second term, Sanders cannot afford a bad result in his home state in 2018.

Although most rural areas in the country voted for Trump, one rare exception was Vermont, the first state "called" by the national networks and the Associated Press, at 7:00 p.m. on November 8, 2016, when we delivered our three electoral votes for the Democratic candidate, not Trump.

So there is hope that Vermont will continue to show that rural America is not in lockstep with Trump.

There is plenty of work to do in our local communities to keep that Vermont "indomitable spirit" alive. We will press ahead, knowing that history is on our side.

Afterword

Jeff Danziger

❧

NON-AMERICANS OFTEN MISS the difference between the states and think of Americans as all pretty much the same. America for them is a blend of bombast, braggadocio, and overweight. The differences between a Mainer and a Los Angeleno are invisible to them. Oddly, this is true even for many Americans. Are Vermonters different from Southerners, Westerners? And in what particulars? I'll repeat the old creak: to a foreigner, a Yankee is an American, to an American a Yankee is a Northerner, to a Northerner a Yankee is a New Englander, to a New Englander a Yankee is a Vermonter, and to a Vermonter a Yankee is a man who eats pie for breakfast.

Some years ago, the Mormons sent a fresh-faced young man named Jim Mullin to Vermont to run for the Senate. He showed up, declared residency, and began spending money in his campaign. The money was from his Mormon backers, including Oren Hatch, still with many rotten tricks in his future. Needless to say, young Mr. Mullin did not appeal to Vermonters, and he failed to be nominated. But some wondered what had given him the idea, or had given his backers their hopes of getting him elected. They had looked at the map, seen an opening, and assumed that states were all pretty much alike. In a small place like Vermont, they reasoned, anyone with some cash could get elected.

And not long ago another transplant, propitiously named McMullen, who was from Massachusetts, made the same mistake. Some will remember that he not only misread the Vermont mind, but he didn't know how many teats a cow had.

The difference between states is a result of history, industry, climate, religion, and a kind of political fog that rises from the earth itself. The same traits are found here and there, but it's the blend of such traits that marks a state's distinctiveness. Vermont's blend is fairness, simplicity, and a strong desire to be left alone. Even the Vermont stereotype is a blend of traits: a laconic sense of humor, taciturn speech, financial tightness, and so on. Most of these are erroneous. But the greatest of these, at least from my observation, is fairness.

Not to patronize my neighbors, but nothing displeases Vermonters more than seeing someone screwed by wealth or power. And this is all the more true when other people are taken advantage of, rather than the Vermonter himself—if that makes sense. If unfairness does occur, then something should be done. If there's no redress, then at least there's widespread rejection.

How then does the state deal with the advance of someone like the current president?

I was living in Plainfield, Vermont, during the Vietnam War, and I received a draft notice in 1966. For reasons I can't remember I obeyed the order, perhaps in part because I had been raised to be an obedient child. I had been taught to think that the United States usually took actions that were fundamentally right, even if the underlying morality was not obvious. I wasn't patriotic, but I wasn't unpatriotic either.

What I wanted most to avoid was the infantry, the destination of nearly all draftees. To escape life slogging around with a rifle, I enlisted and signed up for an assignment to a year-long language school to learn the southern dialect of Vietnamese. The school was housed on a lonely air force base in Texas, on the Mexican border in the most un-Vermont area of the country. At the end of the year, the war was still going on, and my assignment using my new language skills was assured. I had hoped that that the war would end and I would not be needed. But it didn't end.

Thus I wound up in hot, stinking, noisy Vietnam. The army, by that time disorganized and resentful, assigned me to the task

I was least capable of, mechanical maintenance. My unit fixed all sorts of things mechanical, mostly repairing artillery, changing tubes in the guns on the far-flung firebases that were accessible only by helicopter. One can quickly grow uncharmed by helicopters. They are dangerous.

I wrote a letter to George Aiken, as Vermont a person as ever lived. I pointed out that this was a provable waste of taxpayer money, since at some cost and time I had studied the language of our allies, and if we were ever to turn the war over to the South Vietnamese nation, someone would have to tell them. Me, just to take an example. Senator Aiken was famous at the time for suggesting that the way out of the Vietnam quagmire was to simply declare that we had won, and then come home. There was a desperate wit in this solution, and many were impressed by its immediate value.

But the army did not, and still does not, appreciate soldiers getting special attention from their congressmen. I was called into the commander's hut and yelled at. On the table was a letter from George Aiken asking for an explanation or a rectification of this constituent's obviously valid objection. My commander sneered about what would happen if everyone wrote letters to their senator, adding a few sneers about my fitness as an officer. I was a smart guy, wiseass, and so on. Which was pretty accurate. I was hoping to be reassigned to the much safer and air-conditioned headquarters in Saigon, translating stuff. The commander was in a vengeful mood. I wound up working with POWs and intelligence operations, not far from the Cambodian border. So after all my scheming, I was walking around in the jungle with the infantry. And a rifle.

Even so, I will always be grateful to George Aiken. This episode showed me that there was a Vermont identity and that Vermont took care of its own. And since I wasn't killed or wounded, it actually worked out. I wrote a letter of appreciation to Aiken, but kept it brief. No reason to thank someone effusively for doing his job.

I had first fallen in love with the physical beauty of Vermont, but after the war I came home to love the spirit of the place. I taught high school for a number of years, and I noticed that although students left for a while, they often came back. Not for the money, and not for the opportunities to succeed, but for fairness and the shared opinion about what was important in

life. Money was not unimportant, as a friend said, but at best it was just helpful.

So if there is any value in the comparison between, on the one hand, Vermont and its people, and, on the other, a thuggish grifter like Trump, it's that Americans are not all like Trump. Even the people who voted for him are not all like him. Some maybe, but not that many. And for Vermont, a state that, per capita, voted against Trump more than any other state, the way forward is cloudy. If the Trump thugs cut money for schools, kill Obamacare, neglect the infrastructure, and insult Canada in the years to come, how do we react? Many propose that we pay no attention to him. We'll get through the next four years somehow, with inventiveness, cooperation, care for one another, and the sure knowledge that someday it will end and be forgotten, like a storm, powerful but transient.

In other words, as George Aiken advised, we simply declare victory, and come home.

Contributors' Biographies

Julia Alvarez has written novels (*How the García Girls Lost Their Accents, In the Time of the Butterflies, ¡Yo!, In the Name of Salomé, Saving the World*), collections of poems (*Homecoming, The Other Side / El Otro Lado, The Woman I Kept to Myself*), nonfiction (*Something to Declare, Once Upon a Quinceañera, A Wedding in Haiti*), and numerous books for young readers (including the *Tía Lola Stories* series, *Before We Were Free, finding miracles, Return to Sender,* and *Where Do They Go?*). A recipient of a 2013 National Medal of Arts, Alvarez is one of the founders of Border of Lights, a movement to promote peace and collaboration between Haiti and the Dominican Republic. She lives in Vermont.

Al Boright has been satirizing pop song lyrics since the sixth grade. A news junky, Al landed his dream job and then toiled for thirty-one years as one of Vermont's Legislative Counselors. The political insider / wordsmith nature of the job provided just the perch and training for a fertile avocation as a satirist/lyricist/performer. Performances of repurposed tunes have been unleashed at numerous "legislative cabarets," and at the recurring, fake radio show *Ground Hog Opry,* which Al developed with his longtime theatrical partner, George Woodard (together with some dang good Vermont musicians) and which re-emerges for short local springtime tours whenever they feel like it.

Marialisa Calta is a journalist and cookbook author who lives in Calais, Vermont. She once interviewed now-President Trump about an ad he made for Pizza Hut.

Harry Chen, MD, was Commissioner of the Vermont Department of Health from 2011 to 2017. He served in the Vermont House of Representatives from 2002 to 2008. Dr. Chen worked as an emergency physician at Rutland Regional Medical Center for over twenty years, serving as Medical Director from 1998 to 2004. He and his wife Anne raised their three children in Mendon, Vermont.

Jasper Craven is an investigative political reporter whose work has appeared in *Vermont Digger*, the *Boston Globe*, Vermont Public Radio, the *Times Argus*, *Vice*, and others. A Vermont native, he first discovered his love for journalism at the *Caledonian Record*. He double-majored in print journalism and political science at Boston University, and worked in the *Boston Globe*'s Metro and Investigative units. While at the *Globe* he collaborated on "Shadow Campus," a three-part investigative series focused on greed and mismanagement in Boston's off-campus student housing market. The series was a finalist for the 2015 Pulitzer Prize.

Larry Feign is a Goddard College graduate who, through circumstances even he doesn't always understand, ended up becoming a successful cartoonist and writer in Hong Kong, where he lives in a remote village with his wife, dogs, and the occasional uninvited python. However, he always carries a small piece of Vermont in his heart. Experience his website at: larryfeign.com.

Dave Gram recently concluded a more-than-three-decade career as a reporter in the Montpelier bureau of the Associated Press, where one of the things he liked best was the opportunity to try to explain Vermont's quirks to the rest of the world. He wrote a chapter in a 2003 book produced by the *Rutland Herald* and the *Montpelier-Barre Times Argus*, *Howard Dean: A Citizen's Guide to the Man Who Would Be President*. He lives in Montpelier with his wife Cathy; they have two grown sons. Dave's best home brews currently are an oatmeal stout and a Rye-PA.

Joseph F. Hagan Jr., MD, FAAP, is Clinical Professor in Pediatrics and was president of the American Academy of Pediatrics (AAP), Vermont Chapter, as well as chair of several national AAP committees. Dr. Hagan shares weekly coffee and conversation with Bill Mares and practices primary care pediatrics in Burlington, Vermont.

Eric Hanson is a partner in Hanson & Doremus, an investment management firm founded in July 1995. He has managed money in Burlington since 1971. A graduate of St. Lawrence University, Eric is both a chartered financial analyst (CFA) and a certified financial planner. He presently teaches a course, Personal Finance & Investing, at the University of Vermont. Eric has served on the board or as board chair of the Vermont Symphony Orchestra, the Baird Center for Children and Families, the Nature Conservancy, and the Humane Society of Chittenden County. He is presently on the boards of St. Lawrence University, the Vermont Council on World Affairs, Wake Robin, and the Vermont Chinese School. Eric lives in Burlington.

Don Hooper Peace Corps teacher (Botswana '68-'71); Vermont back-to-land goatherd; environmentalist; legislator; Vermont Secretary of State; doodler whose 3 twenty-something sons (Sam, Jay, + Miles) can now surpass him in chainsawing, but not yet in horseshoes. Don is married to Cheese Goddess Allison Hooper, cofounder of the family business Vermont Creamery.

Ed Koren has long been associated with the *New Yorker* magazine, where he has published well over a thousand cartoons as well as many covers and illustrations. He has published six collections of cartoons which first appeared in the *New Yorker*. Koren has received a doctor of humane letters degree from Union College, has been a John Simon Guggenheim Fellow, and a Distinguished Visitor at the American Academy in Berlin. In 2007, he received the Vermont Governor's Award for Excellence in the Arts. Koren was Vermont's Cartoonist Laureate from 2014 to 2017. He is also a member of the Brookfield, Vermont, Volunteer Fire Department. He lives in Vermont with his family.

Madeleine M. Kunin was the governor of Vermont from 1985 to 1991, and she served as United States ambassador to Switzerland from 1996 to 1999. Kunin is the author of *The New Feminist Agenda: Defining the Next Revolution for Women, Work and Family*, a New York Times Editor's Choice selection. Her upcoming memoir, entitled *Coming of Age: My Journey into the Eighties*, is forthcoming (Fall 2018) from Green Writers Press.

Christopher Louras is a native Vermonter who, after graduating from the University of Vermont, served ten years as a US Army CH-47 maintenance manager / maintenance test pilot. He returned to Rutland to raise his family and help his brother and sister run the family business until 2007, when he was elected Mayor of the City of Rutland, serving five terms until his de-election in 2017. He is married to Jude and is the proud father of four sons: Chris, Justin, Ian, and Augie.

Michael Martin, EdD, is the Director of Curriculum & Technology for Montpelier Public Schools and has written over 100 commentaries for Vermont Public Radio on culture and education. He recently wrote *Vermont's Sacred Cow: A Case Study of Local Control of Schools.*

Sally Pollak is a reporter at *Seven Days* in Burlington. Once upon a time she won a big pile of quarters from an A.C. slot machine.

Bill Schubart has lived with his family in Vermont since 1947. Educated locally and at Exeter, Kenyon, and the University of Vermont. He is fluent in French language and culture, which he taught before entering communications as an entrepreneur. He co-founded Philo Records and is the author of the highly successful *Lamoille Stories* (2008), a collection of Vermont tales. His bibliography includes three short-story collections and four novels. He has served on many boards and currently chairs the Vermont College of Fine Arts, known for its writing programs. He speaks extensively on the media and the arts, and writes about Vermont in fiction, humor, and opinion pieces. He is also a regular public radio commentator and blogger. He is the great-great-nephew of the renowned photographer Alfred Stieglitz, and he lives in Vermont with his wife Katherine, also a writer.

Tom Slayton was editor-in-chief of *Vermont Life* magazine for more than twenty years. Prior to that, he was a newspaper writer and editor for the *Rutland Herald*, the *Barre-Montpelier Times Argus*, and the *Boston Globe*. In his retirement he works as a freelance writer and editor, and he is a regular commentator on Vermont Public Radio. Tom has been awarded honorary doctorates of letters by the University of Vermont, Sterling College, and Southern Vermont College. He is a recipient of the Franklin Fairbanks Award, given annually to a Vermonter who contributes in a significant way to the cultural life of the state.

Haviland Smith is a retired CIA station chief who worked in Prague, Berlin, Langley, Beirut, and Tehran, primarily on issues related to the Soviet Union. He also served as chief of the counter-terrorism staff and as executive assistant to the Deputy Director of the Central Intelligence Agency, Frank Carlucci. He is a graduate of Exeter, Dartmouth College, and the University of London. He served in the U.S. Army at the United States Army Security Agency before joining the CIA. He is retired and lives in Williston, Vermont.

Bob Stannard is an eighth-generational Vermonter who has served in the Vermont Legislature, served as a member of the Manchester Selectboard, and served for thirteen years on the Bennington County Regional Planning Commission, three years as chair. He has worked as a lobbyist in Montpelier and a commercial broker with Sotheby's. Bob has been a Vermont columnist for fourteen years and, although retired, he continues to lead one of Vermont's hottest Blues bands, "Downtown" Bob & Those Dangerous Bluesmen. He has produced four CDs and written two Vermont humor books (*How to Survive the Recession* and *How to Survive the Recovery*). He co-wrote *Frankie & Bobby: Growing up Zappa*, a book on the early life of Frank Zappa, with Frank's younger brother, Bobby Zappa. He lives in Manchester, Vermont, with his wife, Alison, of forty-four years.

Stephen C. Terry has had a long career in journalism, business, and managing public affairs strategy in Vermont. He spent sixteen years at the *Rutland Herald*, the last seven as its Managing Editor. Terry worked at Green Mountain Power for twenty-nine years, retiring in 2014 as Senior Vice President. From 1969 to 1975, he served as legislative assistant for U.S. Senator George D. Aiken, R-Vt., during the Vietnam and Watergate Years. He has co-written one book on Aiken and another on the political career of Governor Philip H. Hoff. Terry is now an occasional political analyst for WCAX-TV and WDEV Radio. He lives in Middlebury.

Citizenship Test — ANSWERS

1. C; 2. D; 3. C; 4. (A) VT, (B) NH, (C) VT, (D) NH; 5. Stannard (the Vermont general in command of Union troops who broke Pickett's charge at the Battle of Gettysburg, the decisive battle of the Civil War); 6. B; 7. D; 8. B; 9. B; 10. C. 40; 11. B; 12. (A) New Hampshire, (B) Virginia, (C) New Jersey, (D) Vermont, (E) Florida, (F) Mississippi; 13. (A) *The Good Earth*, (B) *The Ugly American*, (C) *Disappearances*, (D) *In the Fall*, (E) *Understood Betsy*, (F) *The Jungle Books*, (G) *Cancer Ward*; 14. A; 15. B, G, I.

Facts / Alternative Facts Quiz — ANSWERS

1. D; 2. (A) "You may fire when ready . . . ," (B) "Vermont is the most glorious spot . . . ," (C) "I know of no country . . . ," (D) "The best way to kill something . . . ," (E) "Vermont is not for sale," (F) "Either impeach him . . . ," (G) "My idea of a republic . . ."; 3. T; 4. A; 5. B; 6. F; 7. T; 8. T; 9. T; 10. C; 11. (A) Harold Arthur, (B) Lefevre, (C) Bentley, (D) Moulton, (E) Tuttle, (F) Hayden, (G) Lee, (H) Kennedy; 12. None; 13. D; 14. (A) Electric Motor, (B) Platform scale, (C) Steel carpenter's square, (D) Globe; 15. (A) 4, (B) 6, (C) 2, (D) 3, (E) 5, (F) 1

Bill Mares and Jeff Danziger in Vermont.

About the Authors

❧

Raised in Texas, educated at Harvard, **Bill Mares** has been a journalist, a high school teacher, and a member of the Vermont House of Representatives. He has authored or co-authored fifteen books on subjects ranging from the Marine Corps to workplace democracy to presidential fishing, plus four books of humor with Professor Frank Bryan, including the best seller *Real Vermonters Don't Milk Goats*. His hobbies include running, beekeeping, singing and fly fishing. He lives in Burlington, Vermont, with his wife of forty-five years, Chris Hadsel. They have two sons.

Jeff Danziger was born in the Bronx and attended both the University of Vermont and the University of Denver. He served as an intelligence officer in Vietnam, being awarded a Bronze Star and an Air Medal. In 1973 he began drawing for the *Rutland Herald* and *Times Argus*, where he has continued to this day. He also has worked for the *New York Daily News* and the *Christian Science Monitor* and other newspapers. His work has appeared in newspapers around the world from the *Los Angeles Times* to the *London Times* to the *Moscow Times*, and was on the *Washington Post* editorial page of September 12, 2001. He won the Herblock Prize in 2008 and the Thomas Nast Prize (Landau) in 2006. He has published several novels and one children's book. According to John le Carré, "Jeff Danziger is everything a great political cartoonist should be in this over-reverential age: savage, merciless, ribald, and blessed with a lovely eye and hand."